HIPPOCRENE BEGINNER'S SERIES

BEGINNER'S
ARMENIAN

Hagop Andonian

HIPPOCRENE BOOKS
New York

First published as *Modern Armenian* by the Armenian General Benevolent Union of America, 1966.

Copyright © 1999 Hippocrene Books, Inc.

Second printing, 2005.

For information, address:
HIPPOCRENE BOOKS, INC.
171 Madison Avenue
New York, NY 10016
www.hippocrenebooks.com

ISBN 0-7818-0723-9

Printed in the United States of America.

HIPPOCRENE BEGINNER'S SERIES

BEGINNER'S
ARMENIAN

CONTENTS

ERRATA:

1. Page 40, line 20 - Change word *Subjunctive* to *Imperative.*
2. Page 134, line 32 - Change Հայերը մնացին to Հայերը օտր մնացին

Foreword

There is no royal road to learning a language. Mostly a matter of memory, it requires concentration, repetition and constant practice.

This handbook is not a grammar, properly speaking, but it gives the essentials of the modern Western Armenian grammar, together with exercises exemplifying the rules, some conversations with expressions in common usage for practice, and a few pages in prose for reading and translation. It is intended to be a concise presentation of fundamentals which, when mastered, should enable the student to understand the current language fairly well and to express himself clearly in short sentences in an ordinary conversation.

The first step is to learn the alphabet **thoroughly,** to know the sounds of the letters and the way in which they are pronounced in conjunction with others in words.

Then comes the necessity of forming a satisfactory vocabulary. It is said that about six hundred words suffice to cover the needs of daily speech, and that about one thousand words would enable one to read newspapers and speak adequately. The vocabularies (Armenian-English and English-Armenian) given at the end of this book contain approximately twelve to fifteen hundred words each. Nouns—names of objects and abstractions—form the basic structure of speech; hence, their predominance. Then come the operational words: verbs, pronouns, prepositions, adverbs, adjectives, conjunctions, which enable us to form complete sentences with logical, co-ordinated and colorful meaning.

Special effort has been made to avoid going into too many grammatic details and exceptions, and to keep mainly to the basic rules without, however, omitting forms which the student is bound to meet in reading and conversation, and with which, therefore, he should not be altogether unfamiliar.

In order to keep the length of this book within bounds, the examples and exercises given are in Armenian with their English translations; no alternate exercises have been offered in English for translations into Armenian. Instead, it is suggested that the student, at the end of each exercise, translate the English back into Armenian and compare his translation with the text. This has proved to be a practical and helpful method.

Transliteration has not been used because its effectiveness as an aid to pronunciation is limited. A jumble of English letters would be required to indicate some Armenian sounds, and this could easily prove more confusing than helpful. We have therefore relied on the alphabet itself and the examples of English words accompanying it. With rare exceptions, the sounds of the Armenian letters will be exactly the same wherever they appear.

This book, prepared at the suggestion and under the auspices of the Publications Committee of the Armenian General Benevolent Union of America, is principally intended for those of Armenian descent in this country, who have an elementary knowledge of English grammar, and who would like to learn their ancestral language in order to acquire the best direct means of getting acquainted with their rich, cultural heritage. It can, of course, be also used by any English-speaking person who would like to learn modern western Armenian.

New York, 1965.   H. A.

Introduction

Alphabet, Pronunciation, Reading

THE LANGUAGE

Armenians call themselves HAI (pronounced: "High") and their language HAYEREN.

Armenian belongs to the Indo-European group of languages, like Sanskrit, Latin, Persian, Greek, German, English, French. It is written from left to right.

The **written** language has had three phases:

1. **Ancient Armenian** (Grabar) which was in use up to the 19th century beginning with the 5th, when the alphabet was invented by St. Mesrop. This period is rich in religious works, at the head of which is the translation of the Bible, called the "Queen of Translations" because of the beauty and perfection of its language and its fidelity to the text. Ancient Armenian is now used exclusively in the church.

2. **Middle Armenian,** the "Vulgar" or the language of the common people, in which many works have been written from the 12th to the 18th century.

3. **Modern Armenian** (Ashkharabar) which began with the 19th century and has two branches:

    a. the **Western,** based on the Armenian dialect of Constantinople and which is now used by the Armenians in the west.

    b. the **Eastern,** based on the dialect of Yerevan, which is used in Armenia, Persia and India.

The two branches have slight differences in grammar and pronunciation but use essentially the same vocabulary. They are therefore easily understood by both sides.

This book deals with the western modern Armenian.

THE ALPHABET

Print Capital	Lower Case	Armenian Name	English Equivalent	Pronounced as in these words
Ա	ա	ayp	a	car, far, bar
Բ	բ	pen	p	paper
Գ	գ	keem	k	kite
Դ	դ	tah	t	totter
Ե	ե	yech	y (yeh)	yellow
Զ	զ	zah	z	zero
Է	է	eh	e	let, set, yet
Ը	ը	ut	u	utter
Թ	թ	toh	t	totter
Ժ	ժ	zheh	zh	azure
Ի	ի	eenee	e	me, he
Լ	լ	leeoon	l	lily
Խ	խ	kheh	kh	German ch as in "machen"
Ծ	ծ	dzah	dz	madzoon
Կ	կ	guen	g	gold
Հ	հ	ho	h	hat
Ձ	ձ	tsah	ts	tsar
Ղ	ղ	ghad	gh	like the Parisian "r", the German "ch" softened

Print Capital	Lower Case	Armenian Name	English Equivalent	Pronounced as in these words
ծ	ձ	djeh	j	join
Մ	մ	men	m	mummy
Յ	յ	hee	h	harm
Ն	ն	noo	n	none
Շ	շ	shah	sh	share
Ո	ո	vo	v	vocal
Չ	չ	chah	ch	church
Պ	պ	beh	b	baby
Ջ	ջ	cheh	ch	church
Ռ	ռ	rrah	rr	catarrh
Ս	ս	seh	s	sister
Վ	վ	vev	v	very
Տ	տ	deoon	d	do
Ր	ր	reh	r	rare
Ց	ց	tzoh	tz	mezzo
Ւ	ւ	coon	v	avid
Փ	փ	pure	p	paper
Ք	ք	keh	k	king
Օ	օ	o	o	go
Ֆ	ֆ	feh	f	fact

9

THE LETTERS AND THEIR SOUNDS

The Armenian alphabet consists of 38 letters representing vowel sounds and consonants.

VOWELS (Ձայնաւորներ)

The Vowels are: ա, է, ը, ի, օ.

Each letter represents only one sound.

ա – is pronounced as the English letter "a" in: bar, car, father.

Examples

բառ	word	մարմար	marble
տառ	letter	յարմար	suitable
սառ	ice	համար	for
պատ	wall	բառարան	dictionary
պատառ	morsel	վառարան	stove
անտառ	forest	վարժարան	school

է – is pronounced as "e" in: set, get, let.

Examples

սէր	love	էջ	page
դէր	fat	զէնք	weapon
տէր	lord, owner	շէնք	building
կէտ	point	էշ	donkey

NOTE: The letter ե has the vowel sound է in the **middle of words**: մեր our; լեռ mountain; բերել to bring; բեռ load.

ը – is pronounced as "u" in: fur, cur, utter.

Examples

ըսի	I said	ընկեր	companion
ըսաւ	he said	ընտրել	to choose
ըսիք	you said	ընթացք	course
ըսին	they said	ընտանիք	family

The vowel _ը_ often occurs between two consonants though unwritten. Thus: _մկրտել_ is read as if it were written _մըկըրտել_ to baptize; _մրմնջել_ is read like _մըրմընջել._ This unwritten but pronounced _ը_ is called: natural _ը (բնական ը)_ :

_ի_ – is pronounced "ee" as in: me, see, deer.

Examples

_իր_	his, her, its	_իրաւ_	true
դիր	letter	_իմաստ_	meaning
գին	price	_միայն_	alone
գինի	wine	_շիտակ_	straight
գիրք	book	_յիշել_	to remember

_օ_ – is pronounced "_o_" as in: go, more, mode.

Examples

_օդ_	air	_մօտ_	near
_օր_	day	_օրէնք_	law
օրօր	lullaby	_օձ_	snake
օրինակ	example	_օձիք_	collar

Note: The letter _ո_ which is pronounced "vo" at the beginning of words, has the vowel sound "O" in the middle of words.

Examples

որոշ	definite	_գորտ_	frog
դպրոց	school	_որսորդ_	hunter
ցորեն	wheat	_նորոգել_	to renew

VOWEL SOUNDS WITH TWO LETTERS:

There is no single letter in the Armenian alphabet to signify the vowel sound "oo". The letters _ո_ and _ւ_ are put together to represent it: _ու_ (oo)

Examples

_ու_	and	_ուտել_	to eat
տուն	house	_ձուկ_	fish
շուն	dog	_ջուր_	water
կատու	cat	_լուսին_	moon

11

There is no single letter also representing the vowel sound **ü**, as in the French word **pur** or in the German word **müde**. This sound is expressed with the two letters *ի* and *ւ* put together: *իւ*.

Examples

դիւրին	easy	*հիւսիս*	north
բիւրեղ	crystal	*սիւն*	column

The vowel sound, **eu, ö** in the French word **leur**, and in the German word **hören**, does not exist in Armenian words. For purposes of transcribing foreign words with that sound the two letters *է* and *o* are put together: *էo*.

սէոռ	soeur	*էօժէնի*	Eugénie

CONSONANTS (*ԲԱՂԱՁԱՅՆՆԵՐ*)

Certain consonants are pronounced exactly alike by Armenians in the West who no longer sense the difference between them. They retain them, however, in the written language to achieve the correct, traditional spelling. Armenians in the East have preserved the original pronunciation of these letters:

Բ - Փ	pronounced	P	as in **pen**
Գ - Ք	"	K	" **king**
Դ - Թ	"	T	" **taste**
Ձ - Ց	"	TS	" **tsar**
Ջ - Չ	"	CH	" **Church**

Examples

Բ (p)	*բարի* good	*բերան* mouth	*բանալի* key	
Փ	*փակ* closed	*փեթակ* beehive	*փառք* glory	*փեսայ* bridegroom
Գ (k)	*գարուն* spring	*գետ* river	*գարի* barley	*գաւաթ* cup
Ք	*քաջ* brave	*քար* stone	*քեռի* uncle	*քուն* sleep
Դ (t)	*դար* century	*դաշտ* field	*դեռ* yet	*դէմ* against	*դէմք* visage
Թ	*թագ* crown	*թագաւոր* king	*թոռ* grand-child	*թեւ* arm, wing

12

Ձ (ts)	ձագ little one	ձախ left	ձև form	ձի horse	ձիւն snow
8	ցաւ pain	ցամաք land, dry	ցորեն wheat	հաց bread	

Չ (ch)	չար bad	չարիք evil	չարչարել to torture	չեզոք neutral
Ջ	ջուր water	ջերմ warm	ջինջ clear	ջանք effort

Զ (z)	զաւակ child	զուարթ gay	զանազան various	զարդ ornament

Words beginning with the letter զ and followed by ր or ռ, are read as if they are preceded by ը.

Examples

(ը)զբաղիլ to be occupied	(ը)զգացում sentiment	(ը)զգեստ clothing

Ժ (zh) -	ժամ hour	ժամանակ time	ժուժկալ sober	ժիր diligent
Լ (l) -	լեռ mountain	լուր news	լաւ well	լեցուն full
Խ (kh) -	խաւ layer	խաւար dark	խենթ crazy	խելացի intelligent
Ծ (dz) -	ծառ tree	ծով sea	ծոյլ lazy	ծուռ crooked	ծափ clap
Կ (g) -	կաթ milk	կամ or	կարագ butter	կատու cat	կին woman
Հ (h) -	հաց bread	հաւ hen	համար for	հեռու far	հին old
Ղ (gh) -	աղ salt	կաղ lame	դեղ medicine	նեղ narrow	պաղպաղակ ice cream
Ճ (j) -	ճանճ fly	ճագար rabbit	ճերմակ white	ճիշդ correct
Մ (m) -	մարդ man	մաքուր clean	մանուկ child	մելան ink

13

ℰ, յ (h, y) - 1. At the beginning of words this letter has the sound of **h**:

յարմար	յիշել	Յակոբ	յանգ
suitable	to remember	Hagop	rhyme

2. In the middle of words it is pronounced as **y** when it is between two vowels or followed by a consonant:

կայան	կայարան	մայիս	մայր	հայր
halting-place	station	May	mother	**father**

3. At the end of a word it is silent:

վրայ	վկայ	շուկայ	կայ	երեկոյ	անդոյ
on	witness	market	there is	evening	inexistent

ն (n) -

նամակ	նաեւ	նայիլ	նախագահ
letter	also	to look	president

շ (sh) -

շուշան	շաքար	շուն	շողալ
lily	sugar	dog	shine

At the beginning of a word շ if followed by **մ** is read as if it is preceded by an **ը**:

(ը)շտապել	(ը)շտեմարան
to hasten	storehouse

ո (vo) - At the beginning of words it is pronounced **vo**:

որ	որակ	ոգի	որդի
who	quality	spirit	son

But if it is followed by the letter **վ** it loses the initial **v** sound and is read **o**:

In the middle of words, as indicated above, it is pronounced as the vowel **o**:

հով	նորոգել	փոշի	կոտոշ
wind	to renew	powder, dust	horn

ոյ -
(o, ooy) These two letters put together are read as **o** at the end of a word, the letter **յ** being silent as explained above. But if they are followed by a consonant, they are read **ooy**:

14

գոյն	*թոյն*	*բոյն*	*յոյս*
color	poison	nest	hope

քոյր	*բոյր*	*լոյս*	*կոյր*
sister	perfume	light	blind

֊ **(b) -**

պար	*պատ*	*պատիւ*	*պատիժ*	*պետ*
dance	wall	honor	punishment	chief

ռ **(rr) -**

ռամիկ	*ռազմիկ*	*ռահվիրայ*
vulgar	warrior	pioneer

Ս **(s) -**

սառ	*սեռ*	*սարսափ*	*սիրել*
ice	sex, gender	terror	to love

Words beginning with *ս* are read as though the letter *ը* existed before the *ս* when this is followed by any one of the letters *կ*, *պ*, *տ*, *ք* :-

(ը)սկիզբ	*(ը)սպիտակ*	*(ը)սպանել*
beginning	white	to kill

(ը)ստանալ	*(ը)ստուգել*	*(ը)սքանչելի*
to receive	to verify	wonderful

Վ **(v) -**

վարել	*վառել*	*վերմակ*	*վիշտ*
to conduct	to burn	blanket	grief

Տ **(d) -**

տանիլ	*տարբեր*	*տուն*	*տիկին*
to carry	different	house	Mrs., lady

Ր **(r) -**

րոպէ	*մեր*	*ձեր*	*արար*
second	our	your	act

Ւ **(v) -** No word begins with this letter. In the middle of words, between two vowels or after a vowel, it is read as **v**:

գաւաթ	*գաւազան*	*աւազ*	*աւելի*
cup	cane	sand	more

նաւ	*սեւ*	*տերեւ*	*ազնիւ*
boat	black	leaf	noble

We saw that this letter with *ի* forms the diphthong *իւ* pronounced **yoo**. We meet this diphthong in the

15

ending of all abstract nouns in *ուβիւն* which is the equivalent of the English ending ... ation:

բարձրուβիւն	*դիտողուβիւն*	*յայտնուβիւն*	*միուβիւն*
elevation	observation	revelation	union

PUNCTUATION *ԿԷՏԱԴՐՈԻβԻԻՆ*

,	*ստորակէտ*	same as the comma in English.
՚	*բուβ*	placed above the last letter of a word to denote a short stop.
.	*միջակէտ*	corresponding to the semi-colon.
՞	*պարոյկ*	question mark placed on the word.
...	*կախման կէտ*	corresponding to the exclamation point.
՛	*երկար*	interjection sign placed on words of feeling: *ո՛հ, աւա՛ղ.*
։	*վերջակէտ*	corresponding to the English period.
( )	*փակագիծ*	parenthesis.
—	*գծիկ*	to introduce a speaker, also used as parenthesis.
« »	*չակերտ*	quotation marks.
-	*ապաβարձ*	hyphen.

Application of these will be seen in the exercises further on.

SYLLABIFICATION

 Words are divided into syllables in the following mannner:

1. If there is a consonant between two vowels, the consonant passes to the next syllable:

  մա-քուր, փա-փաք, չի-տակ, կա-տու, դու-սան.

2. If there are three consonants at the beginning of a word, the last one passes to the next syllable:

  դր-դել, մր-մունջ, կր-βէչ, փր-կել, βո-չուն.

3. If there are more than one consonant between two vowels, the last one passes to the next syllable:

  բաղ-նիք, մար-դիկ, մար-մին, համ-րել, համ-բոյր.

4. When two succeeding vowels do not form a diphthong, each vowel constitutes a syllable:

  է-ակ, է-ուβ-իւն, Ա-սի-ա, ս-իրէ-ի.

16

Accent

The **tonic accent** in Armenian words is always on the last syllable of the word:

բա—ղո՛ւկ, աք—լո՛ր, պա—տա՛ռ, մա—քո՛ւր, դար—մա՛ն. ա—լա—դա՛ն, դա—լա—դա՛ն, ան—կո—ղի՛ն, թա—դա—ւո՛ր.

The definite article ը at the end of a word is not accented; it is the last syllable of the word itself that bears the accent:

բա—ղո՛ւ—կը, աք—լո՛ր—րը, պա—տա՛—ռը, դար—մա՛—նը. ա—լա—դա՛նը, նա՛—ւը, ա—շո՛ւ—նը, խօ—սի՛—լը.

Capitals

Capital letters are used:

1. The first letter of a sentence: Աստղերը անհամար են:
2. The first letter of each verse: «Ո՛հ, ինչ անուշ եւ ի՛նչպես գով...»
3. All proper nouns: Արշակ, Գրիգոր, Վարդան:
4. The names of peoples: Հայ, Ամերիկացի, Ֆրանսացի, Ռուս:
5. Geographical names: Եւրոպա, Ասիա, Նիւ Եորք, Եփրատ:
6. The word God and its synonyms: Աստուած, Տէր, Արարիչ:

No capital should be used:

If the name of a people is used as an adjective: Հայ զրադէտ մը, յոյն աղջնակ մը:

When an adjective is made from a proper noun: եւրոպական, հայկական, յունական:

The names of religions: քրիստոնէութիւն, մահմետականութիւն:

17

1

Gender, Article, Plural

GENDER

Nouns in Armenian have no gender. We do not have to learn whether **table** is feminine as in French, or **girl** is neuter as in German. Nor do we need to learn masculine, feminine and neuter articles to be used with corresponding nouns. All that is necessary is to learn the words with no concern as to gender.

ARTICLE Յոդ

1. Definite Article

The definite article, corresponding to the English **the,** is the letter ը, added to the word at the end, if the word ends with a consonant; or the letter ն if the word ends with a vowel:

աթոռ	chair	գիրք	book
աթոռը	the chair	գիրքը	the book
գինի	wine	լեզու	tongue
գինին	the wine	լեզուն	the tongue

If the noun ends with a silent յ, the յ is dropped and ն is added:

ճամբայ	road	ապագայ	future
ճամբան	the road	ապագան	the future
հսկայ	giant	ենթակայ	subject
հսկան	the giant	ենթական	the subject

18

If the noun ends with a _ɹ_ that is not silent, the _ɹ_ is retained and _ը_ is added:

Հայ	Armenian	բայը	the verb
Հայը	the Armenian	թէյ	tea
բայ	verb	թէյը	the tea

Words ending with _ւ_ pronounced as **v** also take _ը_ for article:

պատիւ	honor	ցաւ	pain
պատիւը	the honor	ցաւը	the pain

Words ending with consonants may also take **ն** instead of _ը_, if the following word starts with a vowel. In that case the **ն** should be pronounced with the vowel coming after it (liaison):

Հայ–ևու–Յոյնը	the Armenian and the Greek
Հաց–ևու–պանիրը	the bread and the cheese
մարդ–նալ	the man also
որդա–նալ, աղջիկ–նալ	both the boy and the girl
ծառ–նալ, պտուղ–նալ	both the tree and the fruit

Plural of Nouns Յոգնակի

To form the plural of nouns:

a. If the word has one syllable add **եր**:

տուն	house	քար	stone	մարդ	man
տուներ	houses	քարեր	stones	մարդեր	men

b. If the word has more than one syllable add **ներ**:

պարտէզ	garden	աստղ	comet
պարտէզներ	gardens	աստղներ	comets
գնդակ	ball	շուկայ *	market
գնդակներ	balls	շուկաներ	markets

* Note that the silent _ɹ_ at the end of the word is dropped and then **ներ** is added.

19

2. The Indefinite Article

The indefinite article (the English **a** or **an**) is the word մը which is placed after the word separately:

տուն մը   a house   պարտէզ մը   a garden

գնդակ մը   a ball   շուկայ մը   a market

Excercise — Read and translate the following:

շունը, կատուն, բարիկամը, պատկերներ, լապտերները, լուսինը, շուկաներ, վկայ մը, վկաներ, լոյսը, հայրը, հայրերը, առարկայ, առարկաներ, նաւակը, հոգին, սաւան, սաւաններ, գաւազանները, ենթականեր

Note: For the meaning of words not given in the course of the Lessons the Vocabularies at the end of this book should be consulted.

VERB — ԸԼԼԱԼ TO BE

INDICATIVE

Present	**Imperfect**	**Past**
	(Continuous Past)	(Definite)
(ես) եմ I am	էի I was	եղայ I was
(դուն) ես you are	էիր you were	եղար you were
(ան) է he, she, it is	էր he, she, it was	եղաւ he, she, it was
(մենք) ենք we are	էինք we were	եղանք we were
(դուք) էք you are	էիք you were	եղաք you were
(անոնք) են they are	էին they were	եղան they were

The personal pronouns, preceding the verb, are very often omitted as the ending of the verb indicates the person and number of the subject.

The second person singular (դուն, thou) is used only in addressing parents, intimate friends, children, and God in prayer. All other persons should be addressed in the second person plural: դուք, you. This is the polite way.

The Indefinite Article *մը* becomes *մըն* if followed by the verb *եմ*, *ես*, *է*, etc. and the word *ալ* meaning also:

տուն մըն է It is a house

պարտէզ մըն է It is a garden

կին մըն էր It was a woman

տղայ մըն էիր you were a child

թռչուն մըն ալ also a bird

հատ մըն ալ one more

Negative Form

The negative of the present, imperfect and past perfect of *ըլլալ* shown above is obtained by placing the letter *չ* before the verb: *եմ*, *չեմ*:

չեմ I am not	*չէի* I was not	*չեղայ* I was not
չես you are not	*չէիր* you were not	*չեղար* you were not
չէ he, it, she is not	*չէր* he, she, it was not	*չեղաւ* he was not
չենք we are not	*չէինք* we were not	*չեղանք* we were not
չէք you are not	*չէիք* you were not	*չեղաք* you were not
չեն they are not	*չէին* they were not	*չեղան* they were not

Interrogative Form

There is no special form for interrogation. No auxiliary verb is necessary as in English nor inversion as in French. The verb remains as is; only the intonation of the voice indicates the question. The question mark (՞ *պարոյկ*) is placed on the word bearing the question and not at the end of the sentence.

Vocabulary

գիրք book	*ազնիւ* kind	*հոն* there
գրիչ pen	*բարի* good	*շատ* very
մատիտ pencil	*չար* bad	*ինչ* what
թուղթ paper	*ուր* where	*ինչու* why
պզտիկ small	*սիրելի* dear	*ինչպէս* how
մեծ great	*հոս* here	*որովհետեւ* because
բայց but	*եւ, ու* and	

21

Exercise

Տունը մեծ է։   Տունը մե՞ծ է։
The house is big   Is the house big?

Մարդը եւ կինը սիրելի են։
The man and the woman are dear.

Ո՞ւր էիք։   Ո՞ւր են գրիչը եւ մատիտը։
Where were you? Where are the pen and the pencil?

Հոն էի, հոս չէի։   Ինչո՞ւ աղաք չար են։
There I was, here I was not. Why are boys bad?

Որովհետեւ պզտիկ են։
Because they are small.

Conversation

Բարեւ՛	Greetings!
Բարի լոյս, պարո՛ն	Good morning, sir.
Բարի երեկոյ, տիկի՛ն	Good evening, madam.
Գիշեր բարի, օրիո՛րդ	Good night, Miss. . . . .
Ի՞նչպէս էք	How are you?
Շնորհակալ եմ, լաւ եմ	Thank you, I am well.
Դո՞ւք ինչպէս էք	How are you?
Շատ լաւ եմ, շնորհակալ եմ	I am quite well, thank you.
Մնաք բարով Good-bye!	
Յետեսութիւն Au revoir!	Երթաք բարով Good-bye!

2

Noun or Substantive

ԱՆՈՒՆ կամ ԳՈՅԱԿԱՆ

Proper Nouns Յատուկ անուններ

Proper nouns (names of persons, places) begin with a capital letter.

Examples

Արշակ	Յակոբ	Նիւ Եորք	Երեւան	Հայաստան
Arshag	Hagop	New York	Yerevan	Hayasdan

Declension

In Armenian, nouns are declined, that is to say, their endings change according to the function they perform in a sentence. The various forms which they take are called **cases** (հոլովներ).

Thus, to say: **of the house,** instead of using a preposition (**of,** as in English), the word տուն (house) is changed to տունին. Or, to say: **from the house,** instead of using a preposition (**from**), the word տուն is changed to տունէն.

There are six cases:

1. Nominative (ուղղական) - the case of the subject of the sentence.
   Տունը մեծ է, **the house** (subject) is large.

2. Accusative (հայցական) - the case of the direct object.
   Կը սիրեմ տունը, I like **the house** (direct object).

23

3. Genitive (*սեռական*) - case of the possessor, the possessive case. The possessor, whether a person or thing, is always put first:

   Յակոբին տունը   Hagop's house

   Մարդուն աչքը   The man's eye

   Տունին դուռը   Of the house the door

   Աչքին գոյնը   Of the eye the color

4. Dative (*տրական*) - the case of the indirect object, indicating the person or the thing **to** whom or **to** which something is destined:

   The dative form is the same as the **genitive.**

   Արշակին կուտամ   I give **to** Arshag.

5. Ablative (*բացառական*) - the case which shows **from** whom or **from** which the action originates:

   Տունէն կուգամ   I come **from the house.**

6. Instrumental (*գործիական*) - the case which shows **with** what the action takes place:

   Գրիչով կը գրեմ   I write **with** pen.

BASIC FORM OF DECLENSION

	Singular		Plural	
Nom. & Acc.	դաշտ	field	դաշտեր	fields
Gen.	դաշտի	of field	դաշտերու	of fields
Dat.	դաշտի	to field	դաշտերու	to fields
Abl.	դաշտէ	from field	դաշտերէ	from fields
Instr.	դաշտով	with field	դաշտերով	with fields

WITH THE DEFINITE ARTICLE

	Singular		
Nom. & Acc.	դաշտը	դաշտերը	the fields
Gen.	դաշտին	դաշտերուն	of the fields
Dat.	դաշտին	դաշտերուն	to the fields
Abl.	դաշտէն	դաշտերէն	from the fields
Instr.	դաշտովը	դաշտերովը	with the fields

24

Notice that the nominative and accusative, the genitive and dative cases, both in singular and plural, are the same.

There are other forms of declension, mostly inherited from ancient Armenian, which we shall give later on as they are deeply rooted in modern Armenian and the student should therefore know them even though the tendency now is to break away from them as much as possible and to use the basic form of declension.

Vocabulary

գետ	river	ալիք	wave
լեռ	mountain	օդ	air
անտառ	forest	օդանավ	airplane
բնություն	nature	շոգենավ	steamer
լիճ	lake	շոգեկառք	train
երկիր	earth	ճամփորդ	traveler
երկինք	sky, heaven	ճամփորդություն	travel
տիեզերք	universe	արագ	fast
արեգակ, արեւ	sun	դանդաղ	slow
լուսին	moon	բարձր	high
աստղ	star	ցած	low
անջրպետ	space	տկար	weak
ովկիան	ocean	զորավոր	strong
ծով	sea	կլոր	round
անհուն	infinite	այս, այսիկա	this
հեռու	far	այդ, այդիկա	that
մոտ	near	պզտիկ	small
կապույտ	blue	անուշ	sweet
լույս	light	լեղի	bitter

25

Տիեզերքը անհուն է — The universe is infinite

Երկիրը կլոր է — The earth is round

Արեւը մեծ է — The sun is big

Լուսինին լոյսը տկար է — The light of the moon is weak

Լիճին ալիքները պզտիկ են — The waves of the lake are small

Երկինքին գոյնը կապոյտ է — The color of the sky is blue

Օդանաւն ու ինքնաշարժը արագ են — The airplane and the automobile are fast

Շոգենաւն ու շոգեկառքը դանդաղ էին — The steamer and the train were slow

Աստղերը հեռու են բայց լուսինը մօտ է — The stars are far but the moon is near

Ծովին ջուրը անուշ չէ — The water of the sea is not sweet

Բայց գետին ու լիճին ջուրը անուշ է, լեղի չէ — But the water of the river and the lake is sweet, not salty

Շոգենաւով ճամբորդութիւնը հաճելի է — Travel by steamer is agreeable

Note: The order of words in a simple sentence: First the subject, then the attribute and then the verb. In Armenian, as we see from the examples given above the verb comes last contrary to the English wording.

Verb: To be ըլլալ

Future

(Affirmative)		(Negative)	
պիտի ըլլամ	I shall be	պիտի չըլլամ	I shall not be
պիտի ըլլաս	you will be	պիտի չըլլաս	you will not be
պիտի ըլլայ	he, she, it will be	պիտի չըլլայ	he will not be
պիտի ըլլանք	we shall be	պիտի չըլլանք	we shall not be
պիտի ըլլաք	you will be	պիտի չըլլաք	you will not be
պիտի ըլլան	they will be	պիտի չըլլան	they will not be

Note that the negative letter չ is added to the verb and not to the particle պիտի indicating the future tense.

26

Conditional Present

պիտի ըլլայի	I should be
պիտի ըլլայիր	you would be
պիտի ըլլար	he would be
պիտի ըլլայինք	we should be
պիտի ըլլայիք	you would be
պիտի ըլլային	they would be

Conditional Present (negative)

պիտի չըլլայի	I should not be
պիտի չըլլայիր	you would not be
պիտի չըլլար	he would not be
պիտի չըլլայինք	we should not be
պիտի չըլլայիք	you would not be
պիտի չըլլային	they would not be

CONVERSATIONAL

Ի՞նչ է ձեր անունը
What is your name?

Հայերէն գիտէ՞ք
Do you know Armenian?

Այս ձեր գի՞րքն է
Is this your book?

Ո՛չ, բայց պիտի սորվիմ
No, but I shall learn.

Առաջին դասը դժուար է
The first lesson is difficult

Ո՞ւր պիտի ըլլաք
Where will you be?

Ձեր բարեկամը հո՞ս է
Is your friend here?

Ո՛չ, իր եղբայրը հոս է
No, his brother is here.

Հայրը եւ մայրը հոս պիտի ըլլան
The father and the mother will be here.

Ե՞րբ պիտի ըլլան
When will they be?

Ի՞նչ է այս
What is this?

Ասիկա մարդ մըն է
This is a man

Ի՞նչ է այդ
What is that?

Այդ կին մըն է
That is a woman.

or, that can be omitted, it being understood:

Կին մըն է	(It) is a woman
Տղայ մըն է	(It) is a boy
Աղջիկ մըն է	(It) is a girl
Կենդանի մըն է	(It) is an animal

Ի՞նչ կենդանի է այդ What animal is that?	Թռչուն մըն է Միջատ մըն է Շուն մըն է	(It) is a bird (It) is an insect (It) is a dog
Ի՞նչ պտուղ է։ What fruit is (it)?	Նարինջ մըն է Խնձոր մըն է Տանձ մըն է Սեխ մըն է Ձմերուկ մըն է	(It) is an orange (It) is an apple (It) is a pear (It) is a melon (It) is a watermelon
Ո՞վ է այս մարդը։ Who is this man?	Հայ մըն է Ամերիկացի մըն է Անգլիացի մըն է Ֆրանսացի մըն է Իտալացի մըն է Գերմանացի մըն է	(He) is an Armenian (He) is an American (He) is an Englishman (He) is a Frenchman (He) is an Italian (He,) is a German
Ո՞վ է այդ մարդը։ Who is that man?	Արուեստագէտ մըն է Ճարտարապետ մըն է Գրագէտ մըն է Ուսուցիչ մըն է Բանաստեղծ մըն է Երաժիշտ մըն է Գիտնական մըն է Արձանագործ մըն է	(He) is an artist (He) is an architect (He) is a writer (He) is a teacher (He) is a poet (He) is a musician (He) is a scientist (He) is a sculptor
Ո՞ր երկիրն է այդ Which country is that	Այդ երկիրն է Ֆրանսա Թուրքիա Յունաստան Ռուսիա	That country is France Turkey Greece Russia

3

Other Forms of Declension

1. Հայ — Հայու

Singular		**Plural**	
Nom. & Acc. Հայ	Armenian	Հայեր	Armenians
Gen. & Dat Հայու	of, to Armenian Հայերու,	Հայոց	of, to Armenians
Abl. Հայէ	from Armenian Հայերէ		from Armenians
Instr. Հայով	with Armenian Հայերով		with Armenians

The difference from the basic form of declension lies in the genitive and dative cases (singular) which become Հայու instead of Հայի:

The words that are declined after the above form are not many. They are almost all of one syllable. Most of them are declined after the basic form also. They are:

մարդ	man	հով	wind
դար	century	կով	cow
գահ	throne	ծով	sea
արջ	bear	ձի	horse
հաւ	hen	մանչ	boy
նաւ	boat	շահ	profit
արեւ	sun		

The words Հայ and մարդ have also the forms Հայոց, մարդոց, in the genitive and dative plural, along with the usual forms Հայերու, մարդերու:

Հայոց պատմութիւնը - the history of the Armenians.
Մարդոց չարութիւնը - the badness of men.

Examples

արեւուն լոյսը	the light of the sun
ծովուն ալիքնէրը	the waves of the sea
հովուն ձայնը	the sound of the wind
դարուն ոգին	the spirit of the age

All infinitives, when used as nouns, are declined as above:

սիրել – սիրելու, սիրելէ, սիրելով

սիրելու տարիֆը – the age of, to love - the age of loving

սիրելէ դադրիլ – to cease from, to love – to cease loving.

2. *Բարութիւն — բարութեան*

Singular

Nom. & Acc.	բարութիւն	goodness
Gen. & Dat.	բարութեան	of, to goodness
Abl.	բարութենէ	from goodness
Inst.	բարութեամբ	with goodness
	բարութիւնով	

Plural

Nom. & Acc.	բարութիւններ	goodnesses
Gen. & Dat.	բարութեանց	of, to goodnesses
Abl.	բարութիւններէ	from goodnesses
Instr.	բարութիւններով	with goodnesses

All words in իւն are declined as above. These are abstract nouns.

In the plural these words are declined after the basic declension except that in the genitive and dative the ending եանց is used along with the regular երու:- բարութիւններու — բարութեանց:

30

Examples

 գիտութեան ծարաւ
thirst of learning

ազատութեան սէր
love of liberty

ուրախութեան
պատճառ
cause of gladness

Համբերութեամբ
վարուիլ
to act with patience

լռութեամբ
դիտել
to observe with silence

դեղեցկութեան
աղբիւր
source of beauty

ճշմարտութեան սիրահար
lover of truth

թշուառութենէ տառապիլ
to suffer from misery

3. Օր — Օրուան

Singular

Nom. & Acc.	օր - day
Gen. & Dat.	օրուան - of, to day
Abl.	օրէ, օրունէ - from day
Instr.	օրով - with day

The difference from the basic form is in the genitive and dative cases singular which are formed by adding ուան instead of the regular ի.

The plural is formed in accordance with the basic form.

The words declined like օր — օրուան are:

ամիս	առտու	գերեկ	երէկ
month	morning	noon	yesterday
ամառ	տարի	ժամանակ	վաղը
summer	year	time	tomorrow
անգամ	այսօր	իրիկուն	մահ
times	today	evening	death
առաջ	գիշեր	կէսօր	
before	night	noon	

The words ամիս, շաբաթ, ժամանակ, անգամ always follow the basic declension in the ablative case: not ամսունէ, շաբաթունէ, ժամանակունէ, անգամունէ:

In the genitive and dative cases many of these words follow the basic declension.

31

Examples

օրուան ժամերը	դիշերուան լոյսերը
the hours of the day	the lights of the night
առտուընէ ի վեր	երկու անգամուան համար
since morning	for two times
ամառուան օդ	երէկուան լուրը
summer weather	yesterday's news

4. Ճարժում — չարժման

Words ending in ում form their genitive and dative by dropping the ու and adding ան; and their instrumental case by adding ամբ:

Nom. & Acc.	չարժում	movement
Gen. & Dat.	չարժման	of, to movement
Abl.	չարժումէ	from movement
Instr.	չարժմամբ	with movement
	չարժումով	

In the same way are declined դարձարում, անկում, կործանում, etc.

5. Հոգի — Հոգւոյ

Nouns ending with the letters ի and իւ are changed to ւոյ in the genitive and dative cases:

Հոգի – Հոգւոյ	գինի – գինւոյ	եկեղեցի – եկեղեցւոյ
soul - of, to soul	wine - of, to wine	church - of, to church

պատիւ – պատւոյ	հաշիւ – հաշւոյ
honor - of, to honor	account - of, to account

6. Հայր – Հօր

Nom. & Acc.	Հայր	father
Gen. & Dat.	Հօր	of, to father
Abl.	Հօրմէ	from father
Instr.	Հօրմով	with father

The following words are declined in the same way:

մայր	mother	*Սիրամայր*	Mother of God
եղբայր	brother	*Աստուածամայր*	„ „ „
հօրեղբայր	uncle	*նախահայր*	ancestor
մօրեղբայր	uncle	*վանահայր*	abbot
կնքահայր	godfather	*կնքամայր*	godmother

Nom. & Acc.	*քոյր*	sister
Gen. & Dat.	*քրոջ*	of, to sister
Abl.	*քրոջմէ*	from sister
Instr.	*քրոջմով*	with sister

In the same way are declined:

Տէր – տիրոջ	*կին – կնոջ*	*ընկեր – ընկերոջ*
Lord, owner	woman	comrade

8. *Անգլիա – Անգլիոյ*

Nom. & Acc.	*Անգլիա*	England
Gen. & Dat.	*Անգլիոյ*	of, to England
Abl.	*Անգլիայէ*	from England
Instr.	*Անգլիայով*	with England

Words ending in *իա* are declined as above: *Իտալիա*, *Իտալիոյ*; *Ռուսիա*, *Ռուսիոյ*; *Սպանիա*, *Սպանիոյ*:

Names of persons ending in *ա* follow the basic declension, only the letter *յ* is inserted between the vowel *ա* and the next vowel: *Եղիա – Եղիայի*, *Եղիայէ*, *Եղիայով*:

9. *Աղջիկ – Աղջկան*

Nom. & Acc.	*աղջիկ*	girl
Gen. & Dat.	*աղջկան*	of, to girl
Abl.	*աղջկէ*	from girl
Instr.	*աղջկով*	with girl

In the above manner are declined the nouns:

Nom. & Acc. *երիկ* husband *մանուկ – մանկան* child
Gen. & Dat. *երկան* of, to husband *լեռ – լերան* mountain
Abl. *երիկէ* from husband *թոռ – թոռան* grandson
Instr. *երիկով* with husband

All these, however, can be declined after the first basic declension nowadays.

10. *Աստուած – Աստուծոյ*

Nom. & Acc.	*Աստուած*	God
Gen. & Dat.	*Աստուծոյ*	of, to God
Abl.	*Աստուծմէ*	from God
Instr.	*Աստուծմով*	with God

The words *սէր* and *Պոլիս* (Constantinople) follow this declension only in the genitive and dative cases:

սէր love *Պոլիս* Constantinople
սիրոյ of, to love *Պոլսոյ* of, to Constantinople

These words are also declined irregularly:

Սուն and *չուն*, which in the genitive and dative cases, besides the basic forms, have the forms *տան* and *չան*.

Սան դուռը – the door of the house

Շան ձագը – (lit. the little one of the dog) the puppy

The basic forms *տունին* and *չունին* are perfectly correct.

The irregular plurals *մարդիկ* (men) and *տղաք* (children, boys) are declined as follows:

Nom. & Acc.	*մարդիկ*	men	*տղաք*		children
Gen. & Dat.	*մարդոց*	of, to	*տղոց*		of, to
Abl.	*մարդոցմէ*	from	*տղոցմէ*		from
Instr.	*մարդոցմով*	with	*տղոցմով*		with

34

It is a safe rule to follow the forms of the simple basic declension as much as possible. The above irregular forms were indicated here because the student will meet them constantly and they should not puzzle him.

Exercise: On Declensions

Դաշտերուն ծաղիկները գեղեցիկ են – The flowers of the fields are beautiful.

Դարուն յառաջդիմութիւնը – The progress of the century.

Հայոց պատմութիւնը լեցուն է հերոսական արարքներով. The history of the Armenians is full of (with) heroic deeds.

Հօր մը խրատը բարի է – A father's advice is good.

Աղջկան մը սիրտը պաշտելի է – A girl's heart is adorable.

Եղբօրս տունը մօտ է – My brother's house is near.

Երէկուան նամակը կարճ էր – Yesterday's letter was short.

Գիտութեան ուսուցիչները լուրջ մարդիկ են – The teachers of science are serious men.

Իտալիոյ կլիման մեղմ է – The climate of Italy is mild.

Համբերութեամբ սպասեցէք – Wait with patience

Հոգւոյ անմահութիւնը մարդոց սիրելագոյն հաւատքն է – The immortality of soul is the dearest belief of men.

Երկինք կը պատմէ Աստուծոյ փառքը – The heavens declare the glory of God.

Սիրոյ ապացոյցը զոհողութիւնն է – The proof of love is sacrifice.

Մօր մը, կնոջ մը եւ աղջկան մը երազները տարբեր են։
The dreams of a mother, a woman and a girl are different.

Օրուան մը աշխատութիւն ունիմ – I have a day's work.

Մարդոց անգթութիւնը սարսափելի է – The cruelty of men is awful.

Օրէնքները փոփոխման ենթակայ են – Laws are subject to change.

4

Verb: To Have Ունենալ

INDICATIVE MOOD

Affirmative		Negative	
	Present		
ունիմ	I have	չունիմ	I have not
ունիս	you have	չունիս	you have not
ունի	he, she, it has	չունի	he, she, it has not
ունինք	we have	չունինք	we have not
ունիք	you have	չունիք	you have not
ունին	they have	չունին	they have not
	Imperfect		
ունէի	I had	չունէի	I had not
ունէիր	you had	չունէիր	you had not
ունէր	he, she, it had	չունէր	he, she, it had not
ունէինք	we had	չունէինք	we had not
ունէիք	you had	չունէիք	they had not
ունէին	they had	չունէին	you had not

Past Perfect (Affirm.)

ունեցայ	I had
ունեցար	you had
ունեցաւ	he had
ունեցանք	we had
ունեցաք	you had
ունեցան	they had

Past Perfect (Negative)

չունեցայ	I had not
չունեցար	you had not
չունեցաւ	he had not
չունեցանք	we had not
չունեցաք	you had not
չունեցան	they had not

Words

գլուխ	head	*ոսկոր*	bone
դէմք	face	*ծունկ*	knee
ճակատ	forehead	*երակ*	vein
աչք	eye	*շնչերակ*	artery
քիթ	nose	*առողջ*	healthy
բերան	mouth	*հիւանդ*	sick
լեզու	tongue	*ուս*	shoulder
ակռայ	tooth	*սիրտ*	heart
ձեռք	hand	*թոք*	lung
ոտք	foot	*կուրծք*	breast
մարմին	body	*ցաւ*	pain
մատ	finger	*ցաւիլ*	to ache
կոկորդ	throat	*հիմա*	now
անդամ	member	*մէկ*	one
ականջ	ear	*երկու*	two
մորթ	skin		

37

Exercise

Մարմինը անդամներ ունի – The body has members.

* *Քանի՞ գլուխ ունիք* – How many head(s) have you?

Քանի՞ բերան եւ քանի լեզու ունիք – How many mouth (s) and how many tongue(s) have you?

Մէկ գլուխ ունիմ – I have one head.

Մէկ բերան եւ մէկ լեզու ունիմ – I have one mouth and one tongue.

Հիւա՞նդ էք – Are you sick?

Ո՛չ, աղէկ եմ – No, I am well.

Ցաւ ունի՞ք – Have you pain?

Երէկ ցաւ ունէի բայց այսօր ո'չ – Yesterday I had pain but not today.

Մատները պզտիկ են բայց ձեռքերը մեծ – The fingers are small but the hands big.

Քանի՞ սիրտ եւ քանի՞ թոք ունիք – How many heart(s) and how many lung(s) have you?

Մէկ սիրտ ունիմ եւ երկու թոք – I have one heart and two lung(s).

Verbs *ըլլալ, ունենալ*

Compound tense of *ըլլալ* (to be)

Compound tenses are formed with the past participle of the verb and the auxiliary verb which, in Armenian, is the verb **to be** and not **to have**.

The past participle of *ըլլալ* has two forms: *եղած, եղիր*

---

* Note that after *քանի՞* (how many) the noun is not put in plural as in English but in singular.

INDICATIVE

Past Compound

եղած or *եղեր*	*եմ*		I have been
եղած " "	*ես*		you have been
" " "	*է*		he, she, it has been
" " "	*ենք*		we have been
" " "	*եք*		you have been
" " "	*են*		they have been

Pluperfect

եղած or *եղեր*	*էի*		I had been
" " "	*էիր*		you had been
" " "	*էր*		he had been
" " "	*էինք*		we had been
" " "	*էիք*		you had been
" " "	*էին*		they had been

SUBJUNCTIVE

Present

(*որ*) *ըլլամ*	(that)	I be
" *ըլլաս*	"	you be
" *ըլլայ*	"	he, she, it be
" *ըլլանք*	"	we be
" *ըլլաք*	"	you be
" *ըլլան*	"	they be

Past

(*որ*) *եղած* *ըլլամ*	(that)	I have been
" " *ըլլաս*	"	you have been
" " *ըլլայ*	"	he has been
" " *ըլլանք*	"	we have been
" " *ըլլաք*	"	you have been
" " *ըլլան*	"	they have been

Imperfect

(որ)	ըլլայի	(that)	I were
”	ըլլայիր	”	you were
”	ըլլար	”	he were
”	ըլլայինք	”	we were
”	ըլլայիք	”	you were
”	ըլլային	”	they were

Pluperfect

(որ)	եղած	ըլլայի	(that)	I had been
”	”	ըլլայիր	”	you had been
”	”	ըլլար	”	he had been
”	”	ըլլայինք	”	we had been
”	”	ըլլայիք	”	you had been
”	”	ըլլային	”	they had been

Imperative

2nd person singular	(affirmative)	եղիր - Be!
” ” ”	(negative)	մի ըլլար - don't be!
” ” plural	(affirm.)	եղէք - be!
” ” ”	(negative)	մի ըլլաք - don't be.

For the first and third persons the subjunctive is formed by թող .

թող ըլլամ - let me be   թող ըլլայ - let him be
” ըլլանք - let us be   ” ըլլան - let them be

Participles of ըլլալ

Present եղող being
Past եղած or եղեր been
Future ըլլալու, ըլլալիք to be (in the future)

Compound Tenses of ունենալ (to have)

As in the case of the verb **to be**, the compound tenses of ունենալ are formed by combining the past participles of the verb with the auxiliary **to be**. The past participle of ունենալ is: ունեցած or ունեցեր:

INDICATIVE

Past Compound

ունեցած or	*ունեցեր*	*եմ*	I have had
"	"	"	*ես*	you have had
"	"	"	*է*	he, she, it has had
"	"	"	*ենք*	we have had
"	"	"	*եք*	you have had
"	"	"	*են*	they have had

Pluperfect

ունեցած or	*ունեցեր*	*էի*	I had had
"	"	*էիր*	you had had
"	"	*էր*	he had had
"	"	*էինք*	we had had
"	"	*էիք*	you had had
"	"	*էին*	they had had

SUBJUNCTIVE

Present

(*որ*)	*ունենամ*	(that) I have
"	*ունենաս*	" you have
"	*ունենայ*	" he, she, it have
"	*ունենանք*	" we have
"	*ունենաք*	" you have
"	*ունենան*	" they have

Past

(*որ*)	*ունեցած*	*ըլլամ*	(that) I have had
"	"	*ըլլաս*	" you have had
"	"	*ըլլայ*	" he has had
"	"	*ըլլանք*	" we have had
"	"	*ըլլաք*	" you have had
"	"	*ըլլան*	" they have had

41

Imperfect

(որ) ունենայի	(that) I had
" ունենայիր	" you had
" ունենար	" he, she, it had
" ունենայինք	" we had
" ունենայիք	" you had
" ունենային	" they had

Pluperfect

(որ) ունեցած ըլլայի	(that) I had had
" " ըլլայիր	" you had had
" " ըլլար	" he had had
" " ըլլայինք	" we had had
" " ըլլայիք	" you had had
" " ըլլային	" they had had

Imperative

Second person singular	(affirmative)	ունեցի՛ր	have
" " "	(negative)	մի՛ ունենար	do not have
" " plural	ունեցէ՛ք	(affirmative)	have
" " "	(negative)	մի՛ ունենաք	do not have

Participles

Present ունեցող Past ունեցած, ունեցեր
Future ունենալու, ունենալիք

Vocabulary

հայրենիք	fatherland	երկիր	country	քաղաք	city
գիւղ	village	դաշտ	field	ագարակ	farm
ծառ	tree	ծաղիկ	flower	պտոյտ	walk
հաճելի	agreeable, pleasant	երէկ	yesterday	եթէ	if
երբ	when	ուրախ	glad	տխուր	sad

42

ազուոր	pretty	*գեղեցիկ*	beautiful	*ընդարձակ*	vast
կարելի	possible	*անկարելի*	impossible	*հաւանական*	probable
անհաւանական	improbable			*սխալ*	error
անցեալ	past	*միշտ*	always	*օր*	day
շաբաթ	week	*ամիս*	month	*տարի*	year
անցեալ տարի	last year	*առաջ*	before	*ետք*	after
յետոյ	afterward	*վայրկեան*	minute	*այսօր*	today
վաղը	tomorrow	*բոլոր*	all		

Ո՞ւր էիք երէկ։
Where were you yesterday?

Ուրախ պիտի ըլլայի։
I would be glad.

Վաղը հոն պիտի ըլլա՞ք։
Will you be there tomorrow?

Քանի՞ եղբայր ունեցած էք։
How many brother(s) have you had?

Հոս էի երէկ, վաղը հոս պիտի չըլլամ։
I was here yesterday, tomorrow I shall not be here.

Պտոյտը հաճելի՞ էր։
Was the walk pleasant?

Կարելի չէ որ ըլլամ։
It is not possible that I be.

Հաճելի չեղաւ։
It was not pleasant.

Հոս եղա՞ծ էիք։
Had you been here?

Հաւանական է որ ունեցած ըլլա՞ք։
It is probable that you may have had.

5

Verbs ԲԱՅԵՐ

Verbs in Armenian are divided into three groups depending upon the ending of their infinitive. In English the infinitive is recognized by the particle **to** that precedes it: **to** love, **to** sing, etc. In Armenian it is recognized by the ending. These endings are: *ել, իլ, ալ.*

ել - սիրել	to love, to like		*գրել*	to write
իլ - խօսիլ	to speak		*նայիլ*	to look
ալ - կարդալ	to read		*լուալ*	to wash

A verb consists of two parts: the root, which is invariable, and the ending which changes according to the mood, time, person and number. To conjugate a verb is to recite or write these various changes, and these three groups are called conjugations (*խոնարհում-թիւն*):

FIRST CONJUGATION
ԱՌԱՋԻՆ ԼԾՈՐԴՈՒԹԻՒՆ

Infinitive (*անեզբեւոյթ*) ՍԻՐԵԼ

The indicative Present is formed by dropping the ending *ել* and putting instead: *եմ, ես, է, ենք, էք, են,* and the Imperfect by adding: *էի, էիր, էր, էինք, էիք, էին:*

44

The particle *կը* is placed before the verb in the Present and the Imperfect tenses of the Indicative mood (կը *սիրեմ*, կը *սիրէի*) except with the verbs *ըլլալ* (*եմ*, *ես*, *է* etc.), *ունենալ* (*ունիմ*, *ունիս*) which we saw, and *կրնամ* (I can) and *կարծեմ* (I think).

In case the verb starts with a vowel, the *ը* of the particle *կը* is dropped and replaced by an apostrophe('), thus, instead of saying *կը ատեմ*, we must say *կ'ատեմ*, to avoid the clash of the two vowels, *ը* and *ա*, in this case.

INDICATIVE MOOD

Present		Imperfect (Continuing)		Past Perfect	
կը *սիրեմ*	I love	կը *սիրէի*	I loved	*սիրեցի*	I loved
կը *սիրես*	you love	կը *սիրէիր*	you loved	*սիրեցիր*	you loved
կը *սիրէ*	he, she, it loves	կը *սիրէր*	he loved	*սիրեց*	he loved
կը *սիրենք*	we love	կը *սիրէինք*	we loved	*սիրեցինք*	we loved
կը *սիրէք*	you love	կը *սիրէիք*	you loved	*սիրեցիք*	you loved
կը *սիրեն*	they love	կը *սիրէին*	they loved	*սիրեցին*	they loved

Past Compound

սիրած եմ (or *սիրեր եմ*)	I have loved
սիրած ես	you have loved
սիրած է	he, she, it has loved
սիրած ենք	we have loved
սիրած էք	you have loved
սիրած են	they have loved

Pluperfect

սիրած էի	I had loved
սիրած էիր	you had loved
սիրած էր	he had loved
սիրած էինք	we had loved
սիրած էիք	you had loved
սիրած էին	they had loved

Future

պիտի	սիրեմ	I shall love
"	սիրես	you will love
"	սիրէ	he, she, it will love
"	սիրենք	we shall love
"	սիրէք	you will love
"	սիրեն	they will love

Conditional

պիտի	սիրէի	I should love
"	սիրէիր	you would love
"	սիրէր	he would love
"	սիրէինք	we should love
"	սիրէիք	you would love
"	սիրէին	they would love

You will note that the future and the conditional forms are the same as those of the present and imperfect of the indicative except that instead of being preceded by the particle կը, they are preceded by պիտի which is the sign of futurity.

IMPERATIVE MOOD

2nd person singular		սիրէ'	love
" "	plural	սիրեցէ'ք	love
1st "	"	սիրենք	let us love

SUBJUNCTIVE MOOD

The subjunctive forms are the same as those of the indicative mood without the particle կը, but generally introduced by որ or երե:

46

Present (Subjunctive)

(*որ*) *սիրեմ*	(that)	I love
" *սիրես*	"	you love
" *սիրէ*	"	he love
" *սիրենք*	"	we love
" *սիրէք*	"	you love
" *սիրեն*	"	they love

Imperfect

(*որ*) *սիրէի*	(that)	I should love
" *սիրէիր*	"	you would love
" *սիրէր*	"	he would love
" *սիրէինք*	"	we should love
" *սիրէիք*	"	you would love
" *սիրէին*	"	they would love

The subjunctive is used after a verb expressing doubt, an opinion or a wish:

Չեմ կարծեր որ գայ – I don't think that he (will) come.

Կը տարակուսիմ թէ գայ – I doubt that he (will) come.

Պիտի ուզեմ որ նկարէ – I shall wish him to paint.

Պիտի ուզէի որ երգէր – I should wish that he would sing.

Երանի՛ թէ երգէ – Would that he would sing!

Infinitive: *Սիրել* to love, to like.

Participles: Present *սիրող* loving

Past *սիրած*, *սիրեր* loved

Future *սիրելու*, *սիրելիք* to be loved.

All regular verbs ending in *ել* are conjugated according to the above pattern:

գրել	to write	*պարել*	to dance	*լսել*	to hear
երգել	to sing	*գոցել*	to shut	*ծախել*	to sell
շինել	to make	*ընտրել*	to choose	*մարել*	to put out
ղրկել	to send	*նախընտրել*	to prefer	*վառել*	to light
ներել	to forgive	*գնել*	to buy	*շնորհել*	to grant
ներկել	to paint	*ծածկել*	to cover	*խնդրել*	to beg
երազել	to dream	*եփել*	to cook	*ուզել*	to want

Exercise

Կը սիրե՞ք երգել	Do you like to sing?
Կ՚ուզե՞ք պարել	Do you want to dance?
Պիտի ուզէի նկարել	I would like to paint.
Ղրկեցի՞ք գիրքը	Did you send the book?
Կը լսեմ թէ պիտի ղրկէք	I hear that you will send.
Խնդրեցի որ գայ	I asked that he come.
Կը խնդրեմ որ երգէք	I beg that you sing.
Քոյրս եւ ես կ՚երգենք ամէն օր	My sister and I sing every day.
Լսա՞ծ էք թռչունին երգը	Have you heard the bird's song?
Ո՛չ, բայց լսած էի մարդուն երգը	No, but I had heard the man's song.
Դուք երգեցէ՛ք եւ անոնք թող պարեն	You sing and let them dance.
Զարդարեցէ՛ք սենեակը ծաղիկներով	Decorate the room with flowers.

Vocabulary: *Եղանակներ* Seasons

գարուն	spring	*արձակուրդ*	vacation	*Յունուար*	Jan.
ամառ	summer	*երկուշաբթի*	Monday	*Փետրուար*	Feb.
աշուն	autumn	*երեքշաբթի*	Tuesday	*Մարտ*	March

48

ձմեռ	winter	*չորեքշաբթի*	Wednesday	*Ապրիլ*	April
ժամանակ	time	*հինգշաբթի*	Thursday	*Մայիս*	May
տարի	year	*ուրբաթ*	Friday	*Յունիս*	June
ամիս	month	*շաբաթ*	Saturday	*Յուլիս*	July
շաբաթ	week	*կիրակի*	Sunday	*Օգոստոս*	Aug.
օրացոյց	calendar	*ծառ*	tree	*Սեպտեմբեր*	Sept.
ո՞րն է	which is?	*տերեւ*	leaf	*Հոկտեմբեր*	Oct.
որո՞նք են	which are?	*ծաղիկ*	flower	*Նոյեմբեր*	Nov.
եւ այլն	etc.	*պտուղ*	fruit	*Դեկտեմբեր*	Dec.

Conversational

Օրացոյց մը ունի՞ք:
Have you a calendar?

Այո՛, պարոն, ունիմ:
Yes, sir, I have.

Այսօր ի՞նչ օր է:
What day is today?

Այսօր կիրակի է, հանգիստի օր է
Today is Sunday, (it) is day of rest.

Վաղը ի՞նչ օր է:
What day is tomorrow?

*Վաղը երկուշաբթի է, աշխա-
տութեան օր է:*

Tomorrow is Monday, (it) is day
of work.

Երէ՞կ ի՞նչ էր:
What was yesterday?

Երէկ շաբաթ էր:
Yesterday was Saturday.

Տարին քանի՞ եղանակ ունի:
How many seasons has the year?

Տարին չորս եղանակ ունի:
The year has four seasons.

Ո՞ր եղանակները կը սիրէ՞ք:
Which seasons do you like?

Գարունը եւ ամառը:
Spring and summer.

Ո՞րն է արձակուրդի եղանակը:
Which is the season of vacation?

Ամառն է:
It is the summer.

Մառերը ե՞րբ տերեւ կ'ունենան:
When do the trees have leaves?

Գարնան:
In the spring.

Ե՞րբ պտուղ կուտան:
When do they give fruit?

Աշնան:
In the fall.

Որո՞նք են օրերուն անունները:
What are the names of the days?

երկուշաբթի, երեքշաբթի, եւն.:
Monday, Tuesday, etc.

6

Second Conjugation

ԽՕՍԻԼ TO SPEAK

INDICATIVE MOOD

Present

կը	խօսիմ	I speak
"	խօսիս	you speak
"	խօսի	he, she, it speaks
"	խօսինք	we speak
"	խօսիք	you speak
"	խօսին	they speak

Imperfect

կը	խօսէի	I was speaking (used to)
"	խօսէիր	you were speaking
"	խօսէր	he was speaking
"	խօսէինք	we were speaking
"	խօսէիք	you were speaking
"	խօսէին	they were speaking

Perfect

խոսեցայ	I spoke
խոսեցար	you spoke
խոսեցաւ	he spoke
խոսեցանք	we spoke
խոսեցաք	you spoke
խոսեցան	they spoke

Past Compound

խոսած եմ	I have spoken
,, ես	you have spoken
,, է	he, she, it has spoken
,, ենք	we have spoken
,, էք	you have spoken
,, են	they have spoken

Pluperfect

խոսած էի	I had spoken
,, էիր	you had spoken
,, էր	he, she, it had spoken
,, էինք	we had spoken
,, էիք	you had spoken
,, էին	they had spoken

Future

պիտի խոսիմ	I shall speak
,, խոսիս	you will speak
,, խոսի	he, she, it will speak
,, խոսին	we shall speak
,, խոսիք	you will speak
,, խոսին	they will speak

Conditional

պիտի *խօսէի*		I should speak
,,	*խօսէիր*	you would speak
,,	*խօսէր*	he, she, it would speak
,,	*խօսէինը*	we should speak
,,	*խօսէիք*	you would speak
,,	*խօսէին*	they would speak

IMPERATIVE

խօսէ՛ speak (sing.) *խօսի՛նք* let us speak *խօսեցէ՛ք* speak (pl.)

SUBJUNCTIVE

Present

(*որ*) *խօսիմ*	(that)	I speak
,,	*խօսիս*	,, you speak
,,	*խօսի*	,, he, she, it speak
,,	*խօսինք*	,, we speak
,,	*խօսիք*	,, you speak
,,	*խօսին*	,, they speak

Imperfect

(*որ*) *խօսէի*	(that)	I should speak
,,	*խօսէիր*	,, you would speak
,,	*խօսէր*	,, he, she, it would speak
,,	*խօսէինք*	,, we should speak
,,	*խօսէիք*	,, you would speak
,,	*խօսէին*	,, they would speak

Participles

Present - *խօսող* speaking

Past - *խօսած* , *խօսէր* spoken

Future - *խօսելու* , *խօսելիք* to speak (in future), about to speak.

52

Some Verbs of the Second Conjugation:

խորհիլ	to think	մաշիլ	to wear off, to get worn
պատահիլ	to happen	գանգատիլ	to complain
դադրիլ	to cease	վարանիլ	to hesitate
նայիլ	to look	ապրիլ	to live
աշխատիլ	to work	բնակիլ	to dwell, to reside
յոգնիլ	to get tired	պառկիլ	to lie down
փափաքիլ	to wish	սորվիլ	to learn

Exercise

Ի՞նչ կը խորհիք այս մասին	What do you think about this?
Ի՞նչ կը խօսիք այս մասին	What do you speak about this?
Պիտի աշխատիմ Հայերէն սորվիլ	I shall work to learn Armenian.
Պիտի ուզէի լաւ խօսիլ	I should like to speak well.
Շատ աշխատեցայ, յոգնեցայ	I worked much, I got tired.
Կը խօսէի երբ պառկած էիք	I was speaking while you were lying down.
Մի՛ վարանիք, խօսեցէ՛ք	Do not hesitate, speak!
Գրեցի որ խօսի	I wrote that he (should) speak.
Պիտի փափաքէի որ խօսէր	I should like that he speak.
Ո՞ւր կը բնակիք	Where do you live?
Ո՞ւր կը բնակէին իր հայրն ու մայրը	Where did his father and mother live?
Քանի՞ լեզու կը խօսիք	How many languages do you speak?
Հայերէն կը խօսի՞ք	Do you speak Armenian?
Ե՞րբ պիտի սորվիք	When will you learn?
Խօսողը ես եմ	I am the one speaking.

53

Third Conjugation

ԿԱՐԴԱԼ TO READ

INDICATIVE MOOD

Present

կը	կարդամ	I read
″	կարդաս	you read
″	կարդայ	he, she, it reads
″	կարդանք	we read
″	կարդաք	you read
″	կարդան	they read

Imperfect

կը	կարդայի	I was reading (used to)
″	կարդայիր	you were reading
″	կարդար	he was reading
″	կարդայինք	we were reading
″	կարդայիք	you were reading
″	կարդային	they were reading

Perfect

կարդացի	I read
կարդացիր	you read
կարդաց	he read
կարդացինք	we read
կարդացիք	you read
կարդացին	they read

Past Compound

կարդացած	եմ	I have read
″	ես	you have read
″	է	he, she has read
″	ենք	we have read
″	էք	you have read
″	են	they have read

Pluperfect

կարդացած	*էի*	I had read
"	*էիր*	you had read
"	*էր*	he, she had read
"	*էինք*	we had read
"	*էիք*	you had read
"	*էին*	they had read

Future

պիտի	*կարդամ*	I shall read
"	*կարդաս*	you will read
"	*կարդայ*	he, she will read
"	*կարդանք*	we shall read
"	*կարդաք*	you will read
"	*կարդան*	they will read

Conditional

պիտի	*կարդայի*	I should read
"	*կարդայիր*	you would read
"	*կարդար*	he, she would read
"	*կարդայինք*	we should read
"	*կարդայիք*	you would read
"	*կարդային*	they would read

IMPERATIVE

կարդա՛	read (singular)
կարդա՛նք	let us read
կարդացէ՛ք	read (plural)

SUBJUNCTIVE

Present

(*որ*)	*կարդամ*	that I read
"	*կարդաս*	" you read
"	*կարդայ*	" he read

55

(որ) կարդանք   that we read
" կարդաք   " you read
" կարդան   " they read

Imperfect

(որ) կարդայի   that I should read
" կարդայիր   " you would read
" կարդար   " he would read
" կարդայինք   " we should read
" կարդայիք   " you would read
" կարդային   " they would read

Infinitive: կարդալ
Present Participle: կարդացող reading
Past Participle: կարդացած, կարդացեր read
Future Participle: կարդալու, կարդալիք to be read

Some verbs of the Third Conjugation·

ջանալ	to endeavor, try	մնալ	to stay
խաղալ	to play	դոռալ	to thunder
լուալ	to wash	յուսալ	to hope
փութալ	to hasten	մխալ	to fume
տոկալ	to endure	մրմնջել	to murmur

Exercise

Ջանա՛նք հայերէն սորվիլ   Let us endeavor to learn Armenian.
Աշխատի՛նք հայերէն խօսիլ   Let us work to speak Armenian.
Երէկ տունը մնացինք   Yesterday we stayed at home.
Ամպը դոռաց   The cloud thundered.
Ձեր ձեռքերը կը լուա՞ք   Do you wash your hands?
Պիտի գայի եթէ ուզէիք   I would come if you wanted.
Կարդացէ՛ք ձեր դասը   Read your lesson.
Կարդա՛նք միասին   Let us read together.
Վաղը պիտի փութանք գրել   Tomorrow we shall hasten to write.

7

Irregular Verbs

(Անկանոն Բայեր)

All regular verbs are conjugated according to the foregoing three conjugations depending upon their infinitive ending. There are, however, some verbs which do not conform to these three patterns. Some retain their roots but in the past tense, the imperative and the past participle differ from the regular forms. These are called *դարբուղի* (deviating) *բայեր*. There are others which not only differ in the past tense, imperative and past participle but also change their root: these are the Irregular verbs *(անկանոն բայեր)* :

Deviating Verbs of the First Conjugation

Verbs ending with *նել*, such as: *գտ-ն-ել* (to find), *մտ-ն-ել* (to enter), *իջնել* (to descend), *ելլ(ն)ել* (to ascend), *տեսնել* (to see).

In these verbs *ն* which is between the root and the infinitive ending is dropped in the past tense, the imperative and the past participle, thus:

Perfect tense: *գտայ* (I found) *մտայ*, *իջայ*, *ելայ*, *տեսայ*, *ելն*.

Imperative: *գտիր*, *մտիր*, *իջիր*, *ելիր*, *տես*

(pl.) *գտէք*, *մտէք*, *իջէք*, *ելէք*, *տեսէք*.

Past Participle: *գտած*, *մտած*, *իջած*, *ելած*, *տեսած* :

The verbs *առնել* (to take), *խածնել* (to bite), *թքնել* (to spit), *պագնել* (to kiss), become: *առի*, *խածի*, *թքի*, *պագի*.

57

Perfect tense: *առի*, *առիր*, *առաւ* (I took, etc.)

առինք, *առիք*, *առին*:

խածի, *խածիր*, *խածաւ* etc.

պադգի, *պադգիր*, *պադգաւ*, *պադգինք*, etc.

Imperative: *ա՛ռ* (take, sing.)   *խա՛ծ*   *պա՛դ*   *թ՛քի՛ր*

առէ՛ք (take, pl.)   *խածէ՛ք*   *պադէ՛ք*   *թ՛քէ՛ք*

բերել – (to bring) Perfect: *բերի* (I brought), *բերիր*, *բերաւ*,

    (pl.) *բերինք*, *բերիք*, *բերին*·

    Imper. *բե՛ր*, *բերէ՛ք*·

    Past Part. *բերած*, *բերեր*

դնել – (to put) Perfect: *դրի*, *դրիր*, *դրաւ*, *դրինք*, *դրիք*, *դրին*·

    Imper. *դի՛ր*, *դրէ՛ք*

    Past Part. *դրած*, *դրեր*

պարբել – (to hit) Perf. *պարբկի*, *պարբկիր*, *պարբկաւ*

    Imper. *պա՛րկ*, *պարբկէ՛ք*

    Past Part. *պարբկած*, *պարբկեր*

ընել – (to do) Perf. *ըրի* (I did) *ըրիր*, *ըրաւ*, *ըրինք*, *ըրիք*, *ըրին*

    Imper. *ըրէ՛*, *ըրէ՛ք*

    Past Part. *ըրած*, *ըրեր*

ըսել – (to say) Perf. (I said) *ըսի*, *ըսիր*, *ըսաւ*, *ըսինք*, *ըսիք*, *ըսին*

    Imper. *ըսէ՛*, *ըսէ՛ք*

    Past Part. *ըսած*, *ըսեր*

հարցնել – (to ask) Perf. *հարցուցի*, *հարցուցիր*, *հարցուց*,

           հարցուցինք, *հարցուցիք*, *հարցուցին*

    Imper. *հարցո՛ւր*, *հարցուցէ՛ք*

    Past Part. *հարցուցած*, *հարցուցեր*

ցուցնել – (to show), *լեցնել* (to fill), *անցընել* (to make pass)
դարձնել – (to turn), *կորսնցնել* (to lose), as well as all verbs ending in gնել are conjugated like hարցնել:

Excercise

Գտայ մատիտ մը   I found a pencil.

Դուք տեսաք ձեր հայրը   You saw your father.

Շունը խածաւ իր տէրը   The dog bit its master.

58

Ի՞նչ ըսիք	What did you say?
Ըսի ինչ որ երէկ ըրիր	I said what you did yesterday.
Բերէ՛ք գրիչը	Bring the pen.
Դի՛ր մատիտը հոս	Put the pencil here.
Գիրքերն ու լրագիրները առի՞ք	Did you take the books and the newspapers?
Չարկի՞ք թուչունը	Did you hit the bird?
Ի՞նչ ըսաւ	What did he say?
Հարցուցինք եւ պատասխան առինք	We asked and we got (a) reply.
Կորսնցուցի ձեր հասցէն	I lost your address.
Կորսնցուցա՞ծ էք բանալին	Have you lost the key?
Հայրս ու մայրս ցուցուցին ձեր տունը	My father and my mother showed your house.
Դարձուցէ՛ք էջը	Turn the page.

DEVIATING VERBS OF THE SECOND CONJUGATION

Verbs ending in *նիլ* drop the letter *ն* (if it does not belong to the root of the verb) in forming the perfect tense, the imperative and the past participles:

հասնիլ (to arrive): Perfect *հասայ*, *հասար*, *հասաւ* (I arrived, etc.)

(plural) *հասանք*, *հասաք*, *հասան*:

Imper. *հասի՛ր*, *հասէ՛ք*
Past Participle *հասած*, *հասեր*

մեռնիլ (to die): Perf. *մեռայ*, *մեռար*, *մեռաւ* (I died, etc.)

(pl.) *մեռանք*, *մեռաք*, *մեռան*.

Imper. *մեռի՛ր*, *մեռէ՛ք*
Past Part. *մեռած*, *մեռեր*.

ծնիլ (to be born): Perf. *ծնայ*, *ծնար*, *ծնաւ*, *ծնանք*, *ծնաք*, *ծնան*
բուսնիլ (to grow): Perf. *բուսայ*, *բուսար*, *բուսաւ*, etc.

Past Part. *բուսած*, *բուսեր*:

տանիլ (to carry) : Perf. տարի (I carried), տարիր, տարաւ,
                                    տարինք, տարիք, տարին:

Imp. տա՛ր (sing.)   տարէ՛ք (pl.)
     մի՛ տանիր   մի՛ տանիք
     do not carry   do not carry (pl.)

Past Part. տարած, տարէր

հագնիլ (to put on, dress) : Perf. հագայ, հագար, հագաւ, etc.

Imper. հագի՛ր   հագէ՛ք
       մի՛ հագնիր   մի՛ հագնիք

հատնիլ — հատաւ

անցնիլ (to pass, intr.) Perf. անցայ, անցար, անցաւ,
                              անցանք, անցաք, անցան

Imper. անցի՛ր   անցէ՛ք
       մի՛ անցնիր   մի՛ անցնիք

սկսիլ (to begin) Perf. սկսայ, սկսար, սկսաւ,
                       սկսանք, սկսաք, սկսան
Imper. սկսէ՛   սկսեցէ՛ք (pl.)
       մի՛ սկսիր   մի՛ սկսիք
Past. Part. սկսած, սկսէր

նստիլ (to sit), կրթիլ (to break off, snap) are conjugated like
սկսիլ:– նստայ, նստար, նստաւ, etc.

Verbs ending in չիլ:

The letter չ (like ն in հանիլ, մեռնիլ, etc.) is dropped in the
perfect tense, imperative and past participle:
դպչիլ (to touch) Perf. դպայ (I touched), դպար, դպաւ

                        դպանք, դպաք, դպան.
Imper. դպէ՛ր   դպէ՛ք
Past. Part. դպած   դպէր

թռչիլ (to fly), փախչիլ (to flee), փակչիլ (to adhere, stick)
փլչիլ (to crumble) are conjugated like դպչիլ:

A few verbs, however, ending in չիլ and ջիլ like հանգչիլ (to rest),
մարտնչիլ (to struggle), մեղանչիլ (to sin) keep the չ as part
of the root:

60

Perf. Հանգչեցայ (I rested) etc. Հանգչէ՛, Հանգչեցէ՛ք
(rest, imper.)

Մեղանչեցի (I sinned) etc. Մեղանչէ՛, մի՛ մեղանչեր etc.

Exercise

Սկսայ կարդալ	I began to read.
Սկսած եմ կարդալ	I have begun to read.
Վերարկու մը հագայ եւ դուրս ելայ	I put on an overcoat and went out.
Թռչունները թռան	The birds flew.
Պատը փլաւ	The wall crumbled.
Փախի՛ր չար մարդերէն	Flee from bad men.
Քեր փողոցէն անցայ	I passed by your street.
Բայց չտեսայ ձեզ	But I did not see you.
Ե՞րբ սկսաք կարդալ	When did you begin to read?
Երբ խօսիլ սկսայ	When I began to speak.
Թշնամին փախաւ	The enemy fled.
Մենք հասանք, դուք անցաք	We arrived, you passed.
Մանուկ մը ծնաւ	A child was born.
Ե՞րբ հասաք Պոսթընէն	When did you arrive from Boston?
Երբ դուք մեկնեցաք երէկ	When you left yesterday.
Շատ մարդեր մեռան	Many men died.
Եւ շատ մարդեր ծնան	And many men were born.

Vocabulary

ABOUT EATING (ՈՒՏԵԼՈՒ ՄԱՍԻՆ)

ճաշ	meal	կերակուր	food
ճաշել	to dine	սնունդ	nourishment
նախաճաշ	breakfast	աղ	salt
ապուր	soup	պղպեղ	pepper
միս	meat	անուշեղէն	dessert
բանջարեղէն	vegetables	խնձոր	apple
նպարեղէն	groceries	նարինջ	orange
պտուղ	fruit	տանձ	pear

ջուր	water	կեռաս	cherry
կաթ	milk	խաղող	grapes
գինի	wine	շաքար	sugar
գարեջուր	beer	անօթի	hungry
սուրճ	coffee	ծարաւ	thirsty
թէյ	tea	ախորժակ	appetite
պանիր	cheese	կ՚ր հաճի՞ք	will you please
սեղանատուն	dining room	հաճեցէք	please
ճաշարան	restaurant	ներեցէք	excuse me
ուտել	to eat	ալ	too, also
խմել	to drink	ի վեր	since

Conversational

Անօթի եմ	I am hungry.
Ե՛ս ալ անօթի եմ ու ծարաւ	I also am hungry and thirsty.
Ախորժակ ունի՞ք	Have you an appetite?
Այո՛, տեսնե՛նք ճաշացուցակը	Yes, let us see the menu.
Կ՚ր հաճի՞ք ճաշացուցակը բերել	Will you please bring the menu?
Ապուրով մը սկսի՛նք	Let us begin with a soup.
Յետոյ միս եւ բանջարեղէն	Afterwards, meat and vegetables.
Ի՞նչ կ՚ուզէք խմել, գինի՞ թէ գարեջուր	What do you want to drink, wine or beer?
Ջուրը կր նախախնդրեմ	I prefer the water.
Անո՞ւշ բան մը կ՚ուզէք կամ պտուղ	Do you want something sweet or fruit?
Քիչ մը պանիր եւ սուրճ	A little cheese and coffee.
Կր հաճի՞ք հաշիւր բերել	Will you please bring the check?
Ախորժակով կերայ	I ate with appetite.
Հաճոյքով կերայ	I ate with pleasure.
Դարձեալ հրամեցէ՛ք	Come again!

8

Verbs (Continued)

DEVIATING VERBS OF THE THIRD CONJUGATION

Verbs ending in նալ, ենալ, անալ deviate from the regular third conjugation in the perfect tense, imperative and past participle:

բանալ - to open

Perfect: բացի, բացիր, բացաւ․ բացինք, բացիք, բացին
Imperative: բա՛ց, մի՛ բանար․ բացէ՛ք, մի՛ բանաք
Past Participle: բացած, բացեր

դառնալ - to turn. The ռն is changed to րձ.
Perf.: Դարձայ, դարձար, դարձաւ․
դարձանք, դարձաք, դարձան
Imper.: Դարձի՛ր, մի՛ դառնար․ դարձէ՛ք, մի՛ դառնաք
Past Part.: Դարձած, դարձեր
Similarly վերադառնալ (to return), վերադարձայ,
վերադարձար, etc.

իյնալ - to fall
Perf.: Ինկայ, ինկար, ինկաւ․ ինկանք, ինկաք, ինկան
Imper.: Ինկի՛ր, մի՛ իյնար․ ինկէ՛ք, մի՛ իյնաք
Past Part.: Ինկած, ինկեր

$լալ$ - to weep

Perf.: Լացի, լացիր, լացաւ. լացինք, լացիք, լացին
Imper.: Լա՛ց, մի՛ լար. լացէ՛ք, մի՛ լաք
Past Part.: Լացած, լացեր

կենալ - to stay

Perf.: Կեցայ, կեցար, կեցաւ. կեցանք, կեցաք, կեցան
Imper.: Կեցի՛ր, մի՛ կենար. կեցէ՛ք, մի՛ կենաք
Past Part.: Կեցած, կեցեր

մնալ - to remain

Perf.: Մնացի, մնացիր, մնաց, մնացինք, մնացիք, մնացին
Imper.: Մնացի՛ր, մի՛ մնար. մնացէ՛ք, մի՛ մնաք
Past Part.: Մնացած, մնացեր

տալ - to give

Perf.: Տուի, տուիր, տուաւ. տուինք, տուիք, տուին
Imper.: Տո՛ւր, մի՛ տար. տուէ՛ք, մի՛ տաք
Past Part.: Տուած, տուեր

ունենալ - to have

Perf.: Ունեցայ, ունեցար, ունեցաւ.
ունեցանք, ունեցաք, ունեցան
Imper.: Ունեցի՛ր, մի՛ ունենար. ունեցէ՛ք, մի՛ ունենաք.
Past Part.: Ունեցած, ունեցեր

Verbs ending in նալ and անալ are conjugated like կենալ, ունենալ, գիտնալ (to know), ճանչնալ (to recognize).

հասկնալ (to understand)		մոռնալ (to forget)
բարկանալ (to get angry)		հիանալ (to admire)
խոստանալ (to promise)		ստանալ (to receive)

ամչնալ (to be ashamed)
մօտենալ (to approach)
զարմանալ (to wonder)

The verbs *լալ*, *գալ*, *տալ* take the particle *կու* instead of *կը* in the indicative present and imperfect: *կուդամ*, *կուտաք*, *կու-լային*:

Exercise

Ստացայ ձեր նամակը	I received your letter.
Ինչո՞ւ բարկացաք	Why did you get angry?
Քանի՞ օր կեցան	How many days did they stay?
Հոս մնացէ՛ք	Stay here!
Ինչո՞ւ զարմացաք երբ կարդացիք նամակը	Why did you wonder when you read the letter?
Դուռը բացի եւ ներս մտայ	I opened the door and entered.
Գութ ունեցէ՛ք	Have mercy!
Սէր ունեցի՛ր	Have (sing.) love!
Արեւը լոյս եւ ջերմութիւն կու տայ	The sun gives light and heat.
Այս տղաքը ինչո՞ւ կուլան	Why do these boys cry?
Կարդացի եւ հասկցայ	I read and I understood.
Ինչո՞ւ լացին	Why did they weep?
Խոստացէ՛ք եւ տուէ՛ք	Promise and give!
Հայրս վերադարձաւ բայց մայրս հոն մնաց	My father returned but my mother stayed there.
Մօտեցէ՛ք եւ հիացէ՛ք	Approach and admire!

Verbs ending in *ուլ*

There are a few verbs ending in *ուլ* which have a special conjugation. Of these *թողուլ* (to let) is the one most commonly used and in all tenses. The others, like

երդնուլ	(to swear)	*ընթեռնուլ*	(to read)
զբօսնուլ	(amuse oneself)	*զարթնուլ*	(to awake)
ոստնուլ	(to jump)		
զգենուլ	(to put on)		

are used only in the present. Imperfect, futures, and subjunctive present, rather seldom.

65

INDICATIVE

Present	Imperfect	Perfect
կը թողում	կը թողուի	թողուցի
կը թողուս	կը թողուիր	թողուցիր
կը թողու	կը թողուր	թողուց
կը թողունք	կը թողուինք	թողուցինք
կը թողուք	կը թողուիք	թողուցիք
կը թողուն	կը թողուին	թողուցին

Future Present	Future Conditional	Imperative
պիտի թողում	պիտի թողուի	թո՛ղ, մի՛ թողուր
պիտի թողուս	" թողուիր	թողէ՛ք, մի՛ թողուք
պիտի թողու	" թողուր	or թողուցէ՛ք, մի՛ թողուք
պիտի թողունք	" թողուինք	
պիտի թողուք	" թողուիք	
պիտի թողուն	" թողուին	

Pres. Participle: թողող
Past Participle: թողած, թողեր
Future Participle: թողելու, թողելիք

Impersonal Verbs: Անդէմ բայեր

These are verbs of which only the third person singular is used, like:

կ՚անձրեւէ	it rains	կը թուի թէ	it seems that
կը ձիւնէ	it snows	կը կարծուի թէ	it is believed that
կ՚որոտայ	it thunders	կը սառի	it freezes
պէտք է	it is necessary	կը պատահի որ	it happens that

IRREGULAR VERBS

The really irregular verbs, those which change their root in the perfect, imperative and past participle, are:

ուտել - to eat

Perfect: կերայ, կերար, կերաւ. կերանք, կերաք, կերան
Imperative: կե'ր, մի' ուտեր. կերէ'ք, մի' ուտէք
Past Participle: ' կերած, կերեր

երթալ - to go

Perfect: գացի, գացիր, գնաց, գացինք, գացիք, գացին
Imperative: գնա', մի' երթար, գացէ'ք, մի' երթաք
Past Participle: գացած, գացեր

գալ - to come

Perfect: եկայ, եկար, եկաւ., եկանք, եկաք, եկան
Imperative: եկո'ւր, մի' գար, եկէ'ք, մի' գաք
Past Participle: եկած, եկեր

ըլլալ - to be

Perfect: եղայ, եղար, եղաւ. եղանք, եղաք, եղան
Imperative: եղի'ր, մի' ըլլար. եղէ'ք, մի' ըլլաք
Past Participle: եղած, եղեր

Defective Verbs:

The Defective Verbs are those which have no complete conjugation but only some tenses.

1. եմ: It has the Indicative Present and Imperfect as we saw: եմ, ես, է, ենք, էք, են and էի, էիր, էր, էինք, էիք, էին: The other tenses are formed with the help of ըլլալ:

2. կամ: Indic. Pres. կամ, կաս, կայ. կանք, կաք, կան
    Indic. Imperfect: կայի, կայիր, կար.
                      կայինք, կայիք, կային.

Also the present and imperfect of the Subjunctive, same.
Meaning: to be, to exist, կայ - there is. կան - there are:

3. պարտիմ: Ind. Pres. պարտիմ, պարտիս, պարտի, etc.
    Imperfect: պարտէի, պարտէիր, պարտէր, etc.
Meaning: a. to owe. Մէկ տոլար կը պարտիմ ձեզի
                      I owe you one dollar.

    b. to be obliged, must: պարտիմ երթալ
                            I am obliged to, I must **go**.

This idea of obligation, necessity, is rendered more commonly by: պէտf է որ – it is necessary that . . .

պէտք է որ երթամ   I must go
պէտք է որ երթաք   you must go
պէտք է որ գան   they must come

With պէտք է (present indic.) the subjunctive present is used: որ գան, որ երթամ, որ տեսնեն etc.

In the imperfect tense: պէտք էր, the imperfect subjunctive must be used:

պէտք էր որ գային
պէտք էր որ երթային
պէտք էր որ տեսնէին, etc.

Պէտf է **alone,** is followed by the infinitive.

պէտք է երթալ   it is necessary to go
պէտք է կարդալ   it is necessary to read
պէտք է աշխատիլ   it is necessary to work
պէտք էր պայքարիլ   it was necessary to struggle
պէտք էր հնազանդիլ   it was necessary to obey

NEGATIVE VERBS: Ժխտական Բայեր

The negative form of a verb is obtained by adding the letter չ to the verb or to its auxiliary except in the imperative.

տեսնել	to see	չտեսնել	not to see
տեսայ	I saw	չտեսայ	I did not see
սիրած	loved	չսիրած	not loved
խոսած	spoken	չխոսած	not spoken
լսեցի	I heard	չլսեցի	I did not hear

The present and imperfect of the Indicative of a negative verb are formed with the help of the negative present and imperfect of the verb եմ and by changing the last letter of the infinitive *լ* to *ր*:

In the third person singular of the present indicative instead of չէ՛ չի is used: չի սիրեր (he does not love): չի խոսիր (he does not speak); չի կարդար (he does not read).

If the verb starts with a vowel, the *ի* of չի is dropped and replaced by an apostrophe: չառնէք, չ'ունէք, չ'աշխատիր, չ'իմանար:

The second persons of the imperative of negative verbs are formed with the use of մի՛ and the infinitive (the last letter changed to ր) in the case of the second person singular; for the second person plural: մի՛ with the second person plural of the subjunctive:

(sing.) մի՛ սիրեր, մի՛ խօսիր, մի՛ կարդար, մի՛ լսեր, մի՛ տար.
(plur.) մի՛ սիրէք, մի՛ խօսիք. մի՛ կարդաք, մի՛ լսէք, մի՛ տաք
don't love, don't speak, don't read, don't hear, don't give.

CONJUGATION OF A NEGATIVE VERB
Չսիրել – Not to love

Indicative	Future	Subjunctive
		Present
չեմ սիրեր	պիտի չսիրեմ	չսիրեմ
չես սիրեր	պիտի չսիրես	չսիրես
չի սիրեր	պիտի չսիրէ	չսիրէ
չենք սիրեր	պիտի չսիրենք	չսիրենք
չէք սիրեր	պիտի չսիրէք	չսիրէք
չեն սիրեր	պիտի չսիրեն	չսիրեն

Imperfect	Future Conditional	Imperfect
չէի սիրեր	պիտի չսիրէի	չսիրէի
չէիր սիրեր	,, չսիրէիր	չսիրէիր
չէր սիրեր	,, չսիրէր	չսիրէր
չէինք սիրեր	,, չսիրէինք	չսիրէինք
չէիք սիրեր	,, չսիրէիք	չսիրէիք
չէին սիրեր	,, չսիրէին	չսիրէին

Present

չսիրեցի
չսիրեցիր
չսիրեց
չսիրեցինք
չսիրեցիք
չսիրեցին

Imperative

2nd person singular	Pres. Part.	չսիրող
մի՛ սիրեր	Past. ,,	չսիրած
2nd person plural	Future ,,	չսիրելու,
մի՛ սիրէք		չսիրելիք

69

To form the past compound and the pluperfect, the negative form of the verb *եմ* is used with the past participle of the verb in *ած*.

Past Compound

չեմ սիրած	I have not loved
չես սիրած	you have not loved
չէ սիրած	he, she, it has not loved
չենք սիրած	we have not loved
չէք սիրած	you have not loved
չեն սիրած	they have not loved

Pluperfect

չէի սիրած	I had not loved
չէիր սիրած	you had not loved
չէր սիրած	he had not loved
չէինք սիրած	we had not loved
չէիք սիրած	you had not loved
չէին սիրած	they had not loved

Exercise

Չեմ գրեր դասը	I do not write the lesson
Չեմ գրած դասը	I have not written the lesson
Յակոբ չի սիրեր շատ խօսիլ	Hagop does not like to talk much
Արամ չ'ուզեր խաղալ	Aram does not want to play
Գրիգոր լաւ չի լսեր	Krikor does not hear well
Չուզեցիք վերադառնալ	You did not want to return
Չէիք ուզած աշխատիլ	You had not wanted to work
Չ'իմանար ինչ որ կ'ըսէք	He does not hear what you say
Պիտի չաշխատիք միշտ	You will not work always
Գրիգոր երէկ չուզեց խաղալ	Krikor did not want to play yesterday
Այսօր ալ չ'ուզեր խաղալ	Today also he does not want to play
Մի՛ ուտէք, ըսի, ու չկերան	Don't eat, I said, and they did not eat
Չգացի ու չկերայ	I did not go and I did not eat
Չի թողուր որ երթամ	He does not let me go

70

* Զիտղուց որ երթամ*	He did not let me go
Ան չի գար որովհետեւ *չի փափաքիր*	He does not come because he does not desire
Եթէ չգայ, պիտի ցաւիմ	If he does not come, I shall be hurt
* *Եթէ չգար, պիտի ցաւէի*	If he did not come, I should be hurt
Եթէ եկած չըլլար, ցաւած *պիտի ըլլայի*	If he had not come, I should have been hurt

* **Note:** In conditional sentences if the verb in the first clause is in the present, the verb in the second clause must be in future present; if it is in the imperfect, the verb in the second clause must be in conditional present; if in past compound, then the verb in the second clause should be in past conditional.

Passive Verbs: *Կրաւորական Բայեր*

The general rule to change a transitive verb into a passive verb is:

1. To change the infinitive endings *ել* and *իլ* of the first and second conjugations to: *ուիլ*

Examples

սիրել	(to love)	*սիրուիլ*	(to be loved)
կտրել	(to cut)	*կտրուիլ*	(to be cut)
հալածել	(to persecute)	*հալածուիլ*	(to be persecuted)
ընտրել	(to elect)	*ընտրուիլ*	(to be elected)
խօսիլ	(to speak)	*խօսուիլ*	(to be spoken)
շահիլ	(to gain)	*շահուիլ*	(to be gained)

2. In the case of transitive verbs of the third conjugation, the ending *ալ* is changed to: *ացուիլ*.

Examples

կարդալ	(to read)	*խաղալ*	(to play)
կարդացուիլ	(to be read)	*խաղացուիլ*	(to be played)

Those ending in *նալ* are changed to: *ցուիլ*

գող-նալ	(to steal)	*գող-ցուիլ*	(to be stolen)
ճանչ-նալ	(to recognize)	*ճանչ-ցուիլ*	(to be recognized)
գիտ-նալ	(to know)	*գիտ-ցուիլ*	(to be known)

71

All Passive verbs are conjugated after the 2nd Conjugation (like
խոսիլ) :

Indicative Present

կը սիրուիմ	I am loved
կը սիրուիս	you are loved
կը սիրուի	he, she, it is loved
կը սիրուինք	we are loved
կը սիրուիք	you are loved
կը սիրուին	they are loved

Future

պիտի սիրուիմ	I shall be loved
" սիրուիս	you will be loved
" սիրուի, etc.	he will be loved

Future Conditional

պիտի սիրուէի	I should be loved
" սիրուէիր	you would be loved
" սիրուէր	he would be loved
" սիրուէինք, etc.	we should be loved

Imperfect

կը սիրուէի, կը սիրուէիր, etc.	I was loved, etc.

Perfect

սիրուեցայ	I was loved
սիրուեցար	you were loved
սիրուեցաւ	he, she, it was loved
սիրուեցանք	we were loved
սիրուեցաք	you were loved
սիրուեցան	they were loved

Imperative

սիրուէ'	be loved!
սիրուեցէ'ք	be loved! (pl.)
մի' սիրուիք	don't be loved!

Infinitive	*սիրուիլ*
Past Part.	*սիրուած*, *սիրուեր*
Fut. Part.	*սիրուելու*, *սիրուելիք*

The compound tenses of passive verbs are formed, as usual, with the past participle of the verb and the auxiliary:

սիրուած	*եմ*	I have been loved
"	*ես*	you have been loved
"	*է*	he, she, it has been loved
"	*ենք*	we have been loved
"	*էք*	you have been loved
"	*են*	they have been loved
սիրուած	*էի*	I had been loved
"	*էիր*	you had been loved
"	*էր*	he had been loved
"	*էինք*	we had been loved
"	*էիք*	you had been loved
"	*էին*	they had been loved

There are a few verbs which have special passive formations:

տալ	*տրուիլ*	*դնել*	*դրուիլ*	*բանալ*	*բացուիլ*
to give	to be given	to put	to be put	to open	to be opened

ուտել — *ուտուիլ*
to eat - to be eaten; the perfect is *կերուեցայ* (not *ուտուեցայ*):

տանիլ — *տարուիլ*
to carry - to be carried

The preposition **by** used with the passive verbs in English is rendered in Armenian by the ablative case.

Exercise

Հայրերը կը յարգուին	The fathers are respected
Նախագահը կ՚ընտրուի	The President is elected
Մայրերը կը սիրուին	The mothers are loved

73

Այս գիրքը դասատուէս գրուեցաւ	This book was written by my teacher
Նամակը գրուեցաւ.	The letter was written
Նամակը գրուած է	The letter has been written
Ձայնը կը լսուէր	The voice was heard
Դասը դիւրաւ կը կարդացուի	The lesson is read easily
Մայրը կը սիրուի իր տղայէն	The mother is loved by her son
Ծառը իր պտուղէն կը ճանչցուի	The tree is known by its fruit
Թշնամին կը հալածուի զինուորներէն	The enemy is pursued by the soldiers
Գիրքը բացուեցաւ աշակերտէն	The book was opened by the pupil
Ինչ որ կը գրուի, կը կարդացուի	That which is written is read
Հայ գիրերը ՀնարուեցանՍուրբ Մեսրոպէն	The Armenian letters were invented by Saint Mesrop
Հարցումները կը հարցուին ու կը պատասխանուին	The questions are asked and are answered

Causative Verbs - Անցողական Բայեր

These are the verbs the subjects of which make others do the action. It is a form peculiar to the Armenian language and is obtained by adding to the root of a transitive or neuter verb the particle ցնել:

Verbs ending in իլ, change the ի to ե:

խմել	(to drink)	խմցնել	(to make drink)
խօսիլ	(to speak)	խօսեցնել	(to make speak)
կարդալ	(to read)	կարդացնել	(to make read)
մեռնիլ	(to die)	մեռցնել	(to make die, to kill)
քալել	(to walk)	քալեցնել	(to make walk)

Many transitive verbs are made causative not by the particle ցնել but by using the verb տալ:

բանալ տալ	to cause to open
գոցել տալ	to cause to close

74

In conjugating these, only the auxiliary *տալ* is conjugated, the verb itself remains unchanged:

Դուռը բանալ կուտամ	I cause the door to be opened.
Դուռը բանալ պիտի տամ	I shall have the door opened.
Դուռը բանալ տուի	I had the door opened.

The person who is made to do the action of the causative verb is put in the **dative** case:

Դուռը Յակոբին բանալ տուի	I made Hagop open the door.
Հագուստս դերձակին մաքրել տուի:	I made (had) the tailor clean my suit.
Հիւրերուն երգել տուի	I made the guests sing.

Conversational: *Ժամ* (Hour) *եւ* *ժամացոյց* (Watch)

Ժամը քանի՞ է, ժամացոյց ունի՞ք	What time is it? Have you (a) watch?
Ժամը վեցն է, հինգն է, մէկն է	It is six, five, one o'clock.
Վեցին տասը կայ	(There is) It is ten to six.
Վեցին քառորդ կայ	It is a quarter to six.
Վեցը հինգ, տասը կ'անցնի	It is five, ten (minutes) past six.
Վեցը քսան, քսան եւ հինգ կ'անցնի	It is twenty, twenty-five after six.
Վեց ու կէսն է	It is half past six.
Եօթին քսան, քսանեւհինգ կայ	It is twenty, twenty-five to five.
Կէս օր է	It is noon.
Կէս գիշեր է	It is midnight.
Ժամացոյցս ետ կը մնայ	My watch loses.
Ժամացոյցս առաջ կ'երթայ	My watch gains.

9

Adjectives — ածականներ

Adjectives are placed before the noun and remain invariable regardless of the number and case of the noun they qualify. The noun alone is declined both in the singular and plural cases.

Singular

Nom. & Acc.	կարմիր վարդ	red rose
Gen.	կարմիր վարդի	of red rose
Dat.	կարմիր վարդի	to red rose
Abl.	կարմիր վարդէ	from red rose
Instr.	կարմիր վարդով	with red rose

Plural

Nom. & Acc.	կարմիր վարդեր	red roses
Gen.	կարմիր վարդերու	of red roses
Dat.	կարմիր վարդերու	to red roses
Abl.	կարմիր վարդերէ	from red roses
Instr.	կարմիր վարդերով	with red roses

Adjectives do not take articles. The article is affixed to the noun:

կարմիր վարդը the red rose   անոյշ հոտով with the sweet odor
բարձր տունը the high house   սեւ շուներուն to the black dogs

76

Adjectives may be used as nouns and in that case they may take the article, to be declined and be put in plural:

Singular

Nom. & Acc.	*մեծը*	the great
Gen. & Dat.	*մեծին*	of, to the great
Abl.	*մեծէն*	from the great
Instr.	*մեծով*	with the great

Plural

Nom. & Acc.	*մեծերը*	the great ones
Gen. & Dat.	*մեծերուն*	to, of the great ones
Abl.	*մեծերէն*	from the great ones
Instr.	*մեծերովը*	with the great ones

KINDS OF ADJECTIVES

1. Descriptive Adjectives:

These denote a quality of the noun with which they are used:

բարի *մարդ*	good man	կապոյտ *թռչուն*	blue bird
ազնիւ *կին*	kind woman	սիրելի *մայր*	dear mother
մեծ *տուն*	big house	*իմաստուն եւ*	wise and foolish
		յիմար կոյսեր	virgins

Vocabulary:

առաջին	first	*ծեր*	old
վերջին	last	*երիտասարդ*	young
արագ	fast	*խելացի*	intelligent
դանդաղ	slow	*անխելք*	stupid
լեղի	bitter	*կանոնաւոր*	regular
անուշ	sweet	*անկանոն*	irregular
բարի	good	*պաղ*	cold
չար	bad	*տաք*	hot
հաստ	thick	*տխուր*	sad
բարակ	thin	*ուրախ*	glad
տգեղ	ugly	*աղքատ*	poor

ազուոր	pretty	*հարուստ*	rich
աղտոտ	dirty	*երջանիկ*	happy
մաքուր	clean	*դժբախտ*	unhappy
ներկայ	present	*դիւրին*	easy
բացակայ	absent	*դժուար*	difficult
ուղիղ	correct	*արու*	male
սխալ	wrong	*էգ*	female
պարզ	simple	*բաց*	open
բարդ	complicated	*գոց*	closed
կարելի	possible	*նման*	similar
անկարելի	impossible	*տարբեր*	different
չոր	dry	*ողջ*	alive
թաց	wet	*մեռած*	dead
բարձր	high	*իմաստուն*	wise
ցած	low	*յիմար*	foolish
գոհ	satisfied	*կարճ*	short
դժգոհ	dissatisfied	*երկար*	long
թեթեւ	light	*ամուրի*	bachelor
ծանր	heavy	*ամուսնացած*	married

Comparatives:

To form the comparative degree of an adjective:

a. In case of **superiority** the adverb *աւելի* (more) is placed before the adjective, and the noun which is being compared is put in the ablative:

Արամ Գրիգորէն աւելի խելացի է – Aram is more intelligent than Krikor

or, instead of putting the noun compared in the ablative, it is put in the accusative case and preceded by *քան*,

Արամ աւելի խելացի է քան Գրիգորը (accus.)

Նուարդ իր քոյրէն (abl.) *աւելի սիրուն է*

or *Նուարդ աւելի սիրուն է քան իր քոյրը* (accus.)
Nevart is prettier than her sister.

b. In case of **inferiority**, the adverb *նուազ* (less) is used with the ablative, or *քան* with the accusative:

Գրիգոր նուազ խելացի է Արամէն (abl.)
Գրիգոր նուազ խելացի է քան Արամը (accus.)
Krikor is less intelligent than Aram.

c. In case of **equality**, the adverbs, *չափ*, *այնչափ*, *այնքան*, *նոյնչափ*, *նոյնքան*... *որքան* are used:

Գրիգոր Արամին (dative) *չափ խելացի է*
or *Գրիգոր նոյնչափ (as) խելացի է որքան (as) Արամը*:
Krikor is as intelligent as Aram.

The superlative degree of an adjective is obtained by the word *ամէնէն*, the prefix *ամենա* . . . or the suffix . . . *ագոյն*:—

ամէնէն բարձր շէնքը
ամենաբարձր շէնքը   The highest building
բարձրագոյն շէնքը

2. Demonstrative Adjectives:

The Demonstrative Adjectives are: *այս*, this; *այդ*, that; *այն*, that.

They are used with plural nouns also, and in that case mean: these, those.

There is a distinction between *այդ* and *այն*; *այդ* (that) indicates something nearer to the speaker; *այն* (that) farther away.

Examples

այս գիրքը	this book	*այդ մարդը*	that man
այս գիրքերը	these books	*այդ մարդերը*	those men

Note that the definite article is used with the noun; we do not say *այս գիրք*, **but** *այս գիրքը*, *այս լուսերը*:

The demonstrative adjectives are invariable, but the nouns with which they are used may be declined:

Այդ պատկերը գեղեցիկ է   That picture is beautiful.

Այդ նկարին գոյները գեղեցիկ են   The colors of that painting are beautiful.

79

Այս կինը մայրն է այդ տղային	This woman is the mother of that boy.
Այդ խնձորները հասուն են	Those apples are ripe.
Բայց այն դեղձերը խակ են	But those peaches are unripe.
Այս գրիչով կը գրեմ	I write with this pen.
Այդ տուներէն եկան	They came from those houses.
Այս տղան իր եղբայրէն աւելի փոքր է	This boy is smaller than his brother.
Այդ շէնքը աւելի բարձր է քան այս տունը	That building is higher than this house.
Այս գիրքէն աւելի հաշեկան է այդ գիրքը	That book is more interesting than this book.
Այս նկարը ամէնէն գրաւիչն է	This painting is the most attractive.
Այդ դրամը ամենաթանկա-գինն է	That coin is the most precious.
Այս նաւը նոյնքան մեծ է որքան այդ նաւը	This boat is as big as that boat.
Ամէնափոքրը եւ ամենամեծը	The smallest and the greatest.
Թագաւորները ամենազօր էին	The kings were almighty.

3. Numeral Adjectives:

a. Cardinal Numeral Adjectives are:

զերո	0	ութսուն	80
մէկ	1	իննսուն	90
երկու	2	հարիւր	100
երեք	3	հարիւրմէկ	101
չորս	4	երկու հարիւր	200
հինգ	5	երեք հարիւր	300
վեց	6	հազար	1,000
եօթը	7	հազարմէկ	1,001
ութը	8	երկու հազար	2,000
իննը	9	երեք հազար	3,000

տասը	10
տասնըմէկ	11
տասնըերկու	12
տասնըերեք	13
տասնըչորս	14
տասնըհինգ	15
տասնըվեց	16
տասնըեօթր	17
տասնըութր	18
տասնըինը	19
քսան	20
քսանըմէկ	21
երեսուն	30
քառասուն	40
յիսուն	50
վաթսուն	60
եօթանասուն	70

տասը հազար	10,000
քսան հազար	20,000
հարիւր հազար	100,000
մէկ միլիոն	1,000,000

Note: One hundred and **one** thousand are not rendered by *մէկ հարիւր*, *մէկ հազար*, but simply by *հարիւր*, *հազար*.—

Thus:

Հարիւր գիրք ունիմ.
I have one hundred books.

Հազար տոլար ունիմ.
I have one thousand dollars.

Numerals precede the nouns and remain invariable whereas their nouns may be in different cases. They are declined, however, when used as nouns.

The noun after a cardinal number remains in the singular if used in a general sense; it is put in plural if used in a definite sense:

Հինգ տուն	Five house(s)
Ասո՛նք են հինգ տուները	These are the five houses.
Ճամբորդութիւնը վեց օր կը տեւէ	The trip lasts six day(s).
Յիսուն տոլար վճարեցի	I paid fifty dollar(s).

b. **The Ordinal Numbers** are:

առաջին	first
երկրորդ	second
երրորդ	third
չորրորդ	fourth
հինգերորդ	fifth

81

After **fifth,** the suffix _երորդ_ is affixed to the cardinal number to obtain the ordinal:

վեցերորդ	sixth	_տասնեւչորսերորդ_	fourteenth
եօթերորդ	seventh	_քսաներորդ_	twentieth
ութերորդ	eighth	_յիսուներորդ_	fiftieth
իններորդ	ninth	_վաթսուներկուերորդ_	sixty-second
տասներորդ	tenth	_հարիւրերորդ_	hundredth
տասնեւմէկերորդ	eleventh	_հազարերորդ_	thousandth
տասներկուերորդ	twelfth	_երեքհազարերորդ_	three thousandth
տասներեքերորդ	thirteenth		

If the number is compound, the suffix _երորդ_ is affixed to the last number:

Հարիւր եօթանասուն եւ վեցերորդ   one hundred seventy-sixth

չորս Հարիւր վաթսուն եւ մէկերորդ   four hundred sixty-first

In reading common **fractions,** the nominator is read as a cardinal number, and the denominator as an ordinal: 5/8 is read: _հինգ ութերորդ_, ½ - _մէկ երկրորդ_; 2/15 - _երկու տասն եւ հինգերորդ_:

c. Distributive Numerals

These show how many are indicated for each of the nouns they qualify. They are formed, with the exception of one and two by affixing the particle _ական_ to the cardinal number.

երեքական	three each	_տասնական_	ten each
չորսական	four each	_հարիւրական_	one hundred each

In the case of one and two, besides _մէկական_ (one each), the numbers _մէկ_ and _երկու_ are repeated: _մէկ մէկ_, _երկու երկու_, _երկերկու_ and _երկուքական_ are used to mean one each, two each.

Example: _հինգական խնձոր տուինք_ – we gave five apples each.

Exercise·

Այս դասարանին մէջ քսան աշակերտ կայ: There are twenty pupil(s) in this classroom.

Հինգ տոլար եւ քսան սէնթ ունիմ:	I have five dollar(s) and twenty cent(s).
Այս տունին գինը քսան հազար տոլար է:	The price of this house is twenty thousand dollar(s).
Յունիսը տարիին վեցերորդ ամիսն է:	June is the sixth month of the year.
Կարգին առաջինն է:	He is the first of the class.
Տասնական տոլար ստացանք:	We received ten dollars each.
Այս երեք ձիերուն գոյնը ճերմակ է:	The color of these three horses is white.
Քսաներորդ դարը մեծ գիւտերու դարն է:	The twentieth century is the century of great inventions.
Քսաներորդ դարը երկու մեծ պատերազմներու դարն է:	The twentieth century is the century of the two great wars.

4. Possessive Adjectives:

These show to whom a thing belongs. They are:

իմ	my	մեր	our
քու	your	ձեր	your
իր, անոր	his, her, its	իրենց	their

The nouns following these adjectives take as endings the letters ս, դ, ն(ը) according to the person or persons to whom the thing belongs. These letters are called possessive articles. Thus:

my book	իմ գիրքս	our book	մեր գիրքը
your book	քու գիրքդ	your book	ձեր գիրքը
his, her, its book	իր, անոր գիրքը	their book	անոնց իրենց գիրքը

Often the possessive adjectives themselves are omitted. Instead of saying իմ գիրքս we can say գիրքս, the letter ս indicates to whom the thing belongs. If the noun ends with a vowel, of course instead of the letter ը, the letter ն is used: իր ձին, մեր ձին, ձեր կատուն:

If the noun is in the plural the same ending articles are used:

իմ գիրքերս	my books
քու գիրքերդ	your books
իր, անոր գիրքերը	his, her books
մեր գիրքերը	our books
ձեր գիրքերը	your books
անոնց, իրենց գիրքերը	their books

Likewise, the adjectives in the three singular persons may be omitted since the endings clearly indicate to whom the things belong.

The nouns used with or without the possessive adjectives իմ, քու, իր, անոր preceding them are regularly declined as follows:

Singular

Nom. & Acc	(իմ)	գիրքս	my book
Gen. & Dat.	,,	գիրքիս	of, to my book
Abl.	,,	գիրքէս	from my book
Instr.	,,	գիրքովս	with my book

Plural

Nom. & Acc.	(իմ)	գիրքերս	my books
Gen. & Dat.	,,	գիրքերուս	of, to my books
Abl.	,,	գիրքերէս	from my books
Instr.	,,	գիրքերովս	with my books

In the same way are declined:

(քու) գիրքդ	(քու) գիրքերդ
(իր) գիրքը	(իր, անոր) գիրքերը

For the plurals մեր, ձեր, իրենց, անոնց, if omitted, the following suffixes are affixed, for one syllable words:

Instead of saying:				we can say:		
,,	,,	,,	մեր գիրքը,	,,	,,	,, գիրքերնիս
,,	,,	,,	ձեր գիրքը,	,,	,,	,, գիրքերնիդ
,,	,,	,,	իրենց, անոնց գիրքը,	,,	,,	,, գիրքերնին

These are declined as follows:

(Singular and Plural are the same)

Nom. & Acc.	դիրքերնիս	դիրքերնիդ	դիրքերնին
Gen. & Dat.	դիրքերնուս	դիրքերնուդ	դիրքերնուն
Abl.	դիրքերնէս	դիրքերնէդ	դիրքերնէն
Instr.	դիրքերովնիս	դիրքերովնիդ	դիրքերովնին

In the case of words with more than one syllable if the possessive adjectives *մեր*, *ձեր*, *իրենց* are omitted, the noun is declined as follows:

	Singular	**Plural**
Nom. & Acc.	պարտէզնիս	պարտէզներնիս
Gen. & Dat.	պարտէզնուս	պարտէզներնուս
Abl.	պարտէզնէս	պարտէզներնէս
Instr.	պարտէզովնիս	պարտէզներովնիս

It is preferable to avoid using these suffixes especially in the plural cases as they are rather awkward. They are mentioned here so that the student may not be puzzled when he meets them.

Examples

or	իմ տունս ընդարձակ է	My house is large.
	տունս ընդարձակ է	
or	քու սենեակդ պզտիկ է	Your room is small.
	սենեակդ պզտիկ է	
or	իր հայրը ծեր չէ	His, her father is not old
	հայրը ծեր չէ	
or	մեր թռչունը կ՛երգէ	Our bird sings.
	թռչունիս կ՛երգէ	
or	ձեր աղջիկը պիտի գա՞յ	Will your daughter come?
	աղջիկնիդ պիտի գա՞յ	Did you learn your lesson?
	դասդ սորվեցա՞ր	
or	ձեր մայրը հո՞ս է	Is your mother here?
	մայրերնիդ հո՞ս է	

85

Գրիչիս գոյնը կապոյտ է   The color of my pen is blue.

Դասս դժուար է   My lesson is difficult.

Իմ գրիչովս գրէ՛

or գրիչովս գրէ՛   Write with my pen!

5. Indefinite Adjectives:

These are the adjectives which give the noun they qualify a general, vague, **indefinite** meaning. Here are some of them:

ամէն   every (the noun after it must be in the singular)

ամէն մէկ   every one

իւրաքանչիւր   each

բոլոր   all (the noun should be in the plural)

քանի մը, մէկ քանի   a few, several

շատ, շատ մը   many

ուրիշ   other

ո'չ մէկ   not one

որեւէ   any

այսպիսի, այդպիսի   such

ատանկ, ատանկ   such

այսքան, այսչափ   this much

այդչափ   that much

նոյն, միեւնոյն   same

միւս   other

ամբողջ   whole, entire

The following are called interrogative adjectives because they are used in questions:

ո՞ր   which?

ի՞նչ   what?

քանի՞   how many?

ո՞րքան, ի՞նչքան, ո՞րչափ   how much?

ո՞րպիսի, ի՞նչպիսի   what kind of . . .

Examples

Ամէն ծաղիկ հոտ մը ունի	Every flower has an odor.
Իւրաքանչիւր տղայի գիրք մը տուի	I gave a book to each boy.
Նոյն սխալը ըրի	I made the same mistake.
Այսանկ մարդ մը չեմ ճանչցած	I have not known such a man.
Որեւէ պատմութիւն վերջ մը ունի	Any story has an end.
Քանի՞ տուն ունիք	How many houses have you?
Բոլոր պատուհանները գոցեցէ՛ք	Shut all the windows.
Ամբողջ դրամը կորսնցուց	He lost all his money.
Ո՞ր երկիրները այցելած էք	Which countries have you visited?
Ի՞նչ տեսակ մարդ է	What sort of a man is he?
Ո՞ր տունը մեծ է	Which house is big?
Դժուար է այսանկ տուն մը գտնել	It is difficult to find such a house.
Ո՞րչափ դրամ կ'ուզէք	How much money do you want?
Ի՞նչ գրիչ կը գործածէք	What pen do you use?
Քանի՞ մարդ (or hnqh, soul) կայ այս սենեակին մէջ	How many people are there in this room?
Քանի՞ հոգի կը ճանչնաք այստեղ	How many people do you know here?

Possessive adjectives precede the demonstrative adjectives:

Քեր այդ տունը	Your (that) house
Իր այս ընթացքը	His (this) conduct

As seen in the above two examples, while a demonstrative adjective is not used in English with a possessive adjective, in Armenian it is used and it gives an additional meaning: "Your **that** house" not "Your this or the other house." "His this conduct," not his general conduct which may be the meaning of "His conduct," but "His conduct in **this**" particular case.

When a possessive adjective and an indefinite adjective qualify the same noun, the possessive adjective should precede the indefinite:

Իր ո՛չ մէկ գիրքը (not ո՛չ մէկ իր գիրքը) Not one (of) his book (sing.).

Մեր բոլոր տուները ընդարձակ են All our houses are large.

Exercise (On all kinds of adjectives):

Մեծ տուն մը եւ գեղեցիկ պարտէզ մը	A big house and a beautiful garden.
Մեծ տունին դուռը	The door of the big house.
Մեր մեծ տունին դուռը	The door of our big house.
Իմ դուռիս բանալին	The key (of) to my door.
Քու դուռիդ բանալին	The key (of) to your door.
Ձեր պարտէզը աւելի մեծ է մեր պարտէզէն	Your garden is bigger than our garden.
Անոնց տունը աւելի փոքր է քան մեր տունը	Their house is smaller than our house.
Հարիւր ուսանող կայ այստեղ	There are one hundred students here.
Մայրս հրեշտակ մըն է	My mother is an angel.
Ձեր որդին (or որդանիդ) չեկաւ	Your son did not come.
Այս մարդը գուարթ է բայց այդ կինը տխուր է	This man is gay but that woman is sad.
Այս մարդերը երջանիկ են բայց այդ կիները դժբախտ են	These men are happy but those women are unhappy.
Այս երջանիկ մարդիկը կ'աշխատին եւ կը սիրեն իրենց ընտանիքը	These happy men work and love their family.
Ամբողջ քաղաքը	The entire city.
Հարիւրութսունեւութերորդ տարին մեր անկախութեան	The one hundred eighty-eighth year of our Independence.
Այս բարձր, տափակ ու նեղ շէնքը Միացեալ Ազգերու տունն է	This high, flat and narrow building is the home of the United Nations.
Ստացայ իրենց այդ նամակը երկու օր առաջ	I received their (that) letter two days ago.
Ամէն տղայ կը սիրէ խաղալ	Every boy likes to play.

88

Դպրոցին բոլոր տղաքը կը սիրեն
խաղալ

All the boys of the school like to play.

Ո՞ր երգերը կը սիրէք

Which songs do you like?

Ձեր երգերը կը սիրեմ

I like your songs.

Ձեռքերդ մաքո՞ւր են

Are your hands clean?

Անոնց ձեռքերն ալ մաքուր են

Their hands also are clean.

Ամենահարուստ մարդը ամէնէն
երջանիկը չէ

The richest man is not the happiest.

Յաճախ աղքատի մը պէս
դժբախտ է

Often he is unfortunate like a poor man.

Ամէնէն տխուր երգերը ամէնէն
գեղեցիկ երգերն են

The saddest songs are the most beautiful songs.

10

Pronoun — ԴԵՐԱՆՈՒՆ

A pronoun takes the place of a noun. It can therefore like a noun be declined, have person, and number. It is a variable word.

1. Personal Pronouns:

	Singular		Plural	
These are:	ես	I (1st person)	մենք	we
	դուն	you (2nd person)	դուք	you
	ան	he, she, it (3rd person)	անոնք	they

Ես, the pronoun of the **First person,** is declined as follows:

	Singular		Plural	
Nom.	ես	I	մենք	we
Acc.	զիս	me	մեզ	us
Gen.	իմ	of me, my	մեր	of us, our
Dat.	ինծի (ինձ)	to me	մեզի	to us
Abl.	ինձմէ	from me	մեզմէ	from us
Instr.	ինձմով	by, with me	մեզմով	by, with us

90

Դուն, the **Second Person**

	Singular			Plural	
Nom.	*դուն*	you	*դուք*	you
Acc.	*քեզ*	you	*ձեզ*	you
Gen.	*քու*	of you, your	*ձեր*	of you, your
Dat.	*քեզի*	to you	*ձեզի*	to you
Abl.	*քեզմէ*	from you	*ձեզմէ*	from you
Instr.	*քեզմով*	by, with you	*ձեզմով*	by, with you

Ինք, *ան*, *անիկա*, the **Third Person**

Singular

Nom.	*ինք*	*ան*, *անիկա*	he, she, it
Acc.	*զինք*	*զայն*, *զանիկա*	him, her, it
Gen.	*իր*	*անոր*	of him, of her, his, her
Dat.	*իրեն*	*անոր*	to him
Abl.	*իրմէ*	*անկէ*	from him, from her
Instr.	*իրմով*	*անով*	by, with him, her

Plural

իրենք, *անոնք*	they
զիրենք, *զանոնք*	them
իրենց, *անոնց*	of them, their
իրենց, *անոնց*	to them
իրենցմէ, *անոնցմէ*	from them
իրենցմով, *անոնցմով*	by, with them

The third person pronoun (singular and plural) stands for both masculine and feminine nouns, just as in English the third person plural "they" stands both for masculine and feminine nouns and it is from the sense of the sentence that we know to whom they refer.

The personal pronoun is often omitted as subject of the verb, as we saw. "I came", *եկայ* instead of *ես եկայ*.

It is used, however, for emphasis: *Ո՞վ եկաւ*, who came? The answer to this should be *Ե՛ս եկայ*, not simply *եկայ*. The *Ե՛ս* in this case, with an accent, means "It is I who came". Merely *եկայ* would not convey that meaning.

91

Exercise

Գրիգոր ըսաւ ինծի — Krikor said to me.

Ո՞վ տուաւ այդ գիրքը — Who gave that book to you?

Հայրս կը սիրէ զիս — My father loves me.

Իրմէ նամակ մը առի — I received a letter from him.

Տո՛ւր իրեն այս պատկերը — Give him this picture.

Չգրեցի ձեզի — I did not write to you.

Բայց անոնց գրեցի — But I wrote to them.

Անոնք կը խոսին, մենք մուիկ կ'ընենք — They speak, we listen.

Այդ նամակը ձեզմէ եկաւ ինծի — That letter came to me from you.

Քեզմէ առի, քեզի տուի — I took from you, I gave to you.

Գրիչ մը գնեցի, ձեզի տուի զայն երէկ — I bought a pen, I gave it to you yesterday.

Կը սիրենք զիրենք, բայց մօտ չեն մեզի — We love them but they are not near (to) us.

Քեզմէ եկայ, քեզի պիտի վերադառնամ — I came from you, I shall return to you.

Այդ աղջիկը սիրուն է. ան խելացի ալ է — That girl is lovely. She is also intelligent.

Այդ տղան խելացի է, բայց ան չար ալ է — That boy is intelligent, but he is also bad.

Ի՞նչ կը սպասէք ինձմէ կամ իրմէ — What do you expect from me or from him?

Նամակները գրեցի՞ք, ղրկեցի՞ք զանոնք — Did you write the letters? Did you send them?

Reciprocal (Փոխադարձ) and **Reflexive** (Անդրադարձ) Pronouns:

1. Իրար (each other), and մէկզմէկ (one another), which are also personal pronouns, are called **Reciprocal Pronouns**.

These are declined only in the singular as follows:

92

Nom.	None	None
Acc.	*իրար, զիրար*	each other
Gen. & Dat.	*իրարու*	of, to each other
Abl.	*իրարմէ*	from each other
Instr.	*իրարմով*	with each other

Nom.	None	None
Acc.	*մէկզմէկ*	one another
Gen. & Dat.	*մէկմէկու*	of, to one another
Abl.	*մէկմէկէ*	from one another
Instr.	*մէկմէկով*	with one another

Examples

Իրար (զիրար) սիրել	To love each other.
Իրարու գրել	To write to each other.
Իրարմէ զատուիլ	To be separated from each other.
Իրարմով քաջալերուիլ	To be encouraged by each other.
Մէկզմէկ յարգել	To respect one another.
Մէկմէկու օգնել	To help (to) one another.

2. Personal pronouns by repeating themselves once as subject
and then as object (direct or indirect as the verb may govern) form the **Reflexive Pronouns**:- The personal articles
ս for the first person, and *դ* for the second person must be
affixed:

First Person

Singular

Nom.	*Ես ինքս*	I myself
Acc.	*Ես զիս* or *ինքզինքս*	myself
Gen.	*Ես իմ*	I . . . my
Dat.	*Ես ինծի*	I . . . . to me
Abl.	*Ես ինձմէ* or *ինքզինքմէս*	I . . . from myself
Instr.	*Ես ինձմով* or *ինքզինքմովս*	I . . . by, with myself

Plural

Nom.	None	
Acc.	Մենք մեզ or ինքզինքնիս	We ourselves
Gen.	Մենք մեր	We . . . our
Dat.	Մենք մեզի	We . . . to ourselves
Abl.	Մենք մեզմէ	We . . . from ourselves
Instr.	Մենք մեզմով	We . . . with ourselves

Second Person

Singular

Nom.	Դուն ինքդ	you yourself
Acc.	Դուն քեզ or ինքզինքդ	you yourself
Gen.	Դուն քու	you. . . your
Dat.	Դուն քեզի	you to yourself
Abl.	Դուն քեզմէ or ինքնիրմէդ	you from yourself
Instr.	Դուն քեզմով or ինքնիրմովդ	you by, with yourself

Plural

Nom.	None	
Acc.	Դուք ձեզ or ինքզինքնիդ	you . . . yourselves
Gen.	Դուք ձեր	you . . . your
Dat.	Դուք ձեզի	you . . . to yourselves
Abl.	Դուք ձեզմէ	you . . . from yourselves
Instr.	Դուք ձեզմով or ինքիրմովնիդ	you... by, with yourselves

Third Person

Singular

Nom.	None	
Acc.	ինքզինք	him, her, it-self
Gen.	ինքնիր	his, her, its own
Dat.	ինքնիրեն	he . . to himself
Abl.	ինքնիրմէ	he . . . from himself
Instr.	ինքնիրմով	he. . . . by, with himself

Plural

Nom.	None		
Acc.	* իրենք_եզիրենք* or *ինքզինքին*	they . . . themselves
Gen.	*իրենք իրենց*	they . . . their
Dat.	*իրենք իրենց*	they . . . to themselves
Abl.	*իրենք իրենցմէ*	they . . . from themselves
Instr.	*իրենք իրենցմով* or *ինքզիրմովներին*	they . . . by, with themselves

Examples

Ես ինքս գացի եւ ստուգեցի	I myself went and verified.
Դուն քեզ մի՛ խաբեր	Do not deceive yourself.
Ես ինծի կը խօսիմ երբեմն	Sometimes I speak to myself.
Ինքզինքնիդ պատրաստ պա-հեցէ՛ք	Keep yourselves prepared.
Ես ինձմէ գոհ չեմ	I am not satisfied (from) with myself.
Իրենք իրենց արարքով կոր-սնցուցին	They lost by their own deed.
Առանց օգնութեան, մենք մեզ-մով չենք կրնար յաջողիլ այս անգամ :	Without help, we cannot succeed by ourselves this time.
Ես ինձմով հպարտ չեմ	I am not proud of (in Armenian with) myself.
Ինքզինքնիդ (or *դուք ձեզ*) *մի՛ մոռնաք*	Do not forget yourselves.
Դուն քեզ (or *ինքզինքդ*) *կա-ռավարէ՛*	Govern yourself.
Մենք մեզ պիտի պաշտպանենք քաջութեամբ	We shall defend ourselves with courage.

2. Possessive Pronouns: *Ստացական Դերանուններ*

The genitives of personal pronouns are made into possessive pronouns by affixing to them the *ս*, *դ*, *ն* or *ը* articles.

The possessive pronouns are the following:

Singular

1st person	իմս	or	իմ ինս	mine
2nd "	քուկդ	or	քուկինդ	yours
3rd "	իրը	or	իրենը	his

Plural

մերը	or	մերինը	ours
ձերը	or	ձերինը	yours
իրենցը	(seldom իրենցինը)	theirs

The Possessive Pronouns are declined as follows:

	Singular	**Plural**	
Nom. & Acc.	իմս, իմ ինս	իմ իններս	mine
Gen. & Dat.	իմ ինիս	իմ իններուս	of, to mine
Abl.	իմ ինէս	իմ իններէս	from mine
Inst.	իմ ինովս	իմ իններովս	with mine

	Singular	**Plural**	
Nom. & Acc.	մերը, մերինը	մերիններրը	ours
Gen. & Dat.	մերինին	մերիններուն	of, to ours
Abl.	մերինէն	մերիններէն	from ours
Inst.	մերինով	մերիններով	by, with ours

Note that in Armenian the possessive pronouns have different forms for singular and plural, while in English the same pronoun is used for both singular and plural. Thus:

Քեր կատուն ճերմակ է, իմս (or իմ ինս) սեւ է.
Your cat is white, **mine** is black.

Now in the plural:

Քեր կատուները ճերմակ են, իմիննները սեւ են.
Your cats are white, **mine** are black. In English, mine is still used for the plural.

In the same way as իմս are declined:

Քուկդ or քուկինդ (yours), քուկինդ, քուկինէդ, քուկինով.
Ձերը or ձերինը (yours), ձերինին, ձերինէն, ձերինով.
Իրը or իրենը (his), իրենին, իրենէն, իրենով.
Իրենցը or իրենցինը (theirs).

Examples

Իմ գիրքը քու կենէդ աւելի հետաքրքրաշարժ է	My book is more interesting than yours.
Ձեր պարտէզը մերինին մօտ է	Your garden is near (to) ours.
Իմ դասս դժուար է, ձերինը դիւրին է	My lesson is difficult, yours is easy.
Ո՛չ միայն իմ դրամս, իրենն ալ կորսնցուց	Not only my money, he lost his also.
Աս իմ մատիտս է, ո՞ւր է իրենը	This is my pencil, where is his?
Մեր կօշիկները նոր են, ի՞նչ-պէս են ձերինները	Our shoes are new, how are yours?
Եթէ գրիչ չունիք, իմ ինով գրեցէ՛ք	If you have no pen, write with mine.

3. Relative Pronouns:

The relative pronoun "who" or "which" is *որ* when its antecedent - the noun to which it refers - is singular, and *որոնք* when it is plural.

It is declined as follows:

Singular

Nom	որ	who, which
Acc.	զոր	whom, which
Gen. & Dat.	որու	whose, of which, to whom, to which
Abl.	որմէ	from whom, from which
Instr.	որով	with whom, with which

Plural

Nom.	որոնք	who, which
Acc.	զորս	whom, which
Gen. & Dat.	որոնց	whose, of which, to whom, to which
Abl.	որոնցմէ	from whom, from which
Instr.	որոնցմով	with whom, with which

The relative pronoun agrees with its antecedent in number and is put in the case desired according to the function it has in the relative clause:

Ա_յ_դ մ_ա_ր_դ_ը որ կ'ե_ր_թ_ա_յ   That man who goes.

Ա_յ_դ մ_ա_ր_դ_ի_կ_ը դ_ո_ր_ս կ_ը տ_ե_ս_ն_է_ք   Those men whom you see.

Ա_յ_դ ա_ղ_ջ_ի_կ_ն_ե_ր_ը որ_ո_ն_ց ա_ն_ո_ւ_ն_-
ն_ե_ր_ը դ_ի_տ_է_ք   Those girls whose names you know.

Դ_ո_ւ_ն որ ա_շ_խ_ա_տ_ե_լ կ_ը ս_ի_ր_ե_ս...   You who like to work . . .

Often the singular is used, instead of the plural. in the nominative and accusative cases:

Դ_ո_ւ_ք ո_ր (instead of որ_ո_ն_ք) Ե_ւ_ր_ո_պ_ա դ_ա_ց_ի_ք, կ_ը յ_ի_շ_է_ք ա_ն-
շ_ո_ւ_շ_տ...

You, who went to Europe, re member of course . . .

Մ_ե_ն_ք ո_ր (instead of որ_ո_ն_ք) ճ_ա_մ_բ_ո_ր_դ_ե_լ կ_ը ս_ի_ր_ե_ն_ք – դ_ի_տ_ե_ն_ք
թ_է...

We who like to travel, (we) know that . . .

Examples

Գ_ր_ի_չ_ը դ_ո_ր կ_ը բ_ո_ն_ե_մ   The pen which I hold.

Տ_ղ_ա_ն ո_ր կ_ը կ_ա_ր_դ_ա_յ   The boy who reads.

Ա_յ_դ տ_ե_տ_ր_ա_կ_ը որ_ո_ւ_ն դ_ո_յ_ն_ը
կ_ա_ն_ա_ն_չ է   That book the color of which is green.

Ս_ի_ր_տ_ը ո_ր_մ_է ա_ր_ի_ւ_ն կ_ը հ_ո_ս_ի   The heart from which blood flows.

Մ_ա_տ_ի_տ_ն_ե_ր_ը որ_ո_ն_ց_մ_ո_վ կ_ը դ_ր_ե_ն_ք   The pencils with which we write.

Կ_ի_ն_ը որ_ո_ւ_ն դ_ի_ր_ք_ը կ_ա_ր_դ_ա_ց_ի_ք   The woman whose book you read.

Տ_ղ_ա_ն որ_ո_ւ_ն խ_ա_ղ_ա_լ_ի_ք մ_ը տ_ո_ւ_ի   The boy to whom I gave a toy.

Ա_յ_ն ա_ն_ձ_ը որ_ո_ւ_ն տ_ո_ւ_ի_ք ձ_ե_ր
ք_ո_ւ_է_ն   The person to whom you gave your vote (for whom you voted).

Դ_ո_ւ_ք ո_ր կ_ը ս_ի_ր_ե_ք կ_ա_ր_դ_ա_լ   You who like to read.

Ձ_ե_դ ո_ր տ_ե_ս_ա_ն_ք...   You whom we saw . . .

Շ_ո_ւ_ն_ը դ_ո_ր կ_ը տ_ե_ս_ն_է_ք, մ_ե_ր_ի_ն_ն է   The dog which you see is ours.

4. Demonstrative Pronouns: Ց_ո_ւ_ց_ա_կ_ա_ն Դ_ե_ր_ա_ն_ո_ւ_ն_ն_ե_ր

These are the same as the Demonstrative Adjectives except that they do not accompany a noun but a verb. They are declined:

98

Singular

Nom. & Acc.	*այս, ատ, ատիկա*	this
Gen. & Dat.	*ատոր*	of this, to this
Abl.	*ատկէ*	from this
Instr.	*ատով*	with this

Plural

Nom. & Acc.	*ատոնք*	these
Gen. & Dat.	*ատոնց*	of these, to these
Abl.	*ատոնցմէ*	from these
Instr.	*ատոնցմով*	with these

այդ, ատոնք and *այն, անոնք* are declined like *այս.*

Examples

Քեր դիրքը լաւ է, անով *գոհացէ՛ք*	Your position is good, be satisfied with it.
Այս է մեր կարծիքը	This is our opinion.
Քեր գո՞րծն է այդ	Is that your work?
Չէի տեսած ատիկա	I had not seen it.
Այս տղաքը կ՛աշխատին, ա— նոնցն է ապագան	These boys work, theirs is the future.
Այդ է մեր որոշումը	That is our decision.
Այս տղոց հայրը ատոնց հօրեղբայրն է	The father of these boys is the uncle of those.
Ասկէ աւելի մեծ է	It is bigger than this.

5. Indefinite Pronouns: *Անորոշ Դերանուններ*

Most of the Indefinite Adjectives when used without nouns become pronouns. They generally take the definite article (*ը, ն*) and accompany verbs.

ամէնը, ամէնքը	all
ամէն մէկը, իւրաքանչիւրը	each one
մէկ քանին	a few
ո՛չ մէկը, ո՛չ ոք	none, no one

99

նոյնը, միևնոյնը	the same
բոլորը	all
այսքանը, այսչափը	this much
ինչ	what
ինչ որ	which
մարդ	one
ուրիշ, ուրիշ մը	other, another
շատեր	many
քիչ մը	a little
քիչեր	few
մէկը եւ միւսը	the one and the other
ոչինչ	nothing
բան մը	something
ամէն բան	everything
ո՞վ	who?
ո՛վ որ	whoever

Most of the Indefinite Pronouns are declined according to the First Basic Declension. Exceptions: ամէն մէկը, ո՛չ մէկը, ո՞ր մէկը, մարդ, which are declined like: ծով, ծովու: Ամէն մէկուն:

Examples

Մէկը կ՚աշխատի, միւսը կը դիտէ	The one works, the other watches.
Մէկուն տուին, միւսէն առին	They gave to one, they took from the other.
Իւրաքանչիւրին մէկ տօլար տուին	They gave one dollar to each.
Ո՛չ ոք կ՚ուզէ հիւանդանալ	Nobody wants to get sick.
Ո՞վ է այն մարդը որ պիտի չուզէր ապրիլ	Who is the man who would not like to live?
Ոչինչ այնքան կը սիրեմ որքան կարդալ	I like nothing so much as to read.
Քիչեր գիտեն առողջութեան յարգը	Few know the value of health.

Այս գլխարկներէն ո՞րը կը
նախընտրէք

Which of these hats do you prefer?

Այս հինգ գիրքերէն ո՞րը
կարդացիք

Which of these five books did you read?

Պաշտպանէ՛ իրաւունքդ եւ
յարգէ՛ ուրիշներունը

Defend your right and respect that of others.

Ամէն մէկուն համ մը տուի

I gave one to each.

Ամէն մէկէն համ մը առի

I took one from each.

Ի՞նչ գիտէք — ոչինչ գիտեմ

What do you know? I know nothing.

Ինչ որ ցանես զայն կը հնձես

That which you sow, that (is what) you reap.

Ուրիշի մի վստահիր դիւրաւ

Do not trust (to) others easily.

Այդ պտուղներէն ինծի ալ քիչ
մը տո՛ւր

Give me also some of those fruits.

Երեք մատիտ ունիմ, ո՞րը
կ՚ուզէք

I have three pencils, which one do you want?

Ամէն ծառ արմատ, ճիւղեր եւ
շատ տերեւներ կ՚ունենայ

Every tree has root, branches and many leaves.

Ամէնուն մէջէն այս մէկր
ընտրեցի

I selected this one from among them all.

Մարդ միշտ յոյսով կ՚ապրի

One lives always with hope.

Ո՛չ ոքի հետ խոսեցայ

I spoke with no one.

Դուք ամէնուն հետ խոսեցաք

You spoke with everybody.

11

Prepositions — ՆԱԽԱԴՐՈՒԹԻՒՆՆԵՐ

In modern Armenian few are the prepositions which, as their name implies, precede the noun or pronoun which they govern; most of them follow the noun or pronoun and are therefore postpositions really. Prepositions and postpositions govern different cases.

1. **Prepositions:**

   a. Dative case:

   առանց   without

առանց ջուրի	without water
առանց հագուստի	without clothing
առանց ինձի	without me

   փոխանակ   instead of

փոխանակ դրամի	instead of money
փոխանակ գալու, գնաց	instead of coming, he went

   b. Accusative case:

դէպի	toward	դէպի տուն	toward home
մինչեւ	until, also as far as	մինչեւ իրիկուն	until evening
		մինչեւ կայարան	as far as the station
իբր, իբրեւ	as	իբր նուէր	as gift

102

b. Ablative case:

բացի except

բացի կիներէն   except the women.
բացի ինձմէ ամէն մարդ հոն էր   everybody was there except me.

2. Postpositions:

a. Genitive:

առջեւ	in front of	տունին առջեւ	in front of the house.
ետեւ	behind	դուռին ետեւ.	behind the door.
տակ	under	աթոռին տակ	under the table.
վրայ	on	սեղանին վրայ	on the table.
մէջ	in	սենեակին մէջ	in the room.
մէջտեղ	middle	սրահին մէջտեղը	in the middle of the room.
միջեւ	between	իր եւ իմ միջեւ	between him and me.
շուրջ	around, about	քաղաքին շուրջ	around the city.
տեղ	instead of	կաթի տեղ ջուր տուաւ	instead of milk he gave water.
դիմաց	opposite, vis-a-vis	Ձեր տունը մեր տան դիմաց է	Your house is opposite our house
մասին	regarding, about	Ձեր մասին խոսեցաւ	He spoke about you.

b. Dative:

համար	for	ինձի համար	for me.
		Յակոբին համար	for Hagop.
հակառակ	contrary, despite	իր խոսստումին հակառակ	contrary to his promise.
հետ	with	հօրը հետ	with his father.
համեմատ համաձայն }	according	Գրոյցի մը համեմատ	according to a rumor.
		Մեր խոստումին համաձայն	according to our promise.
հանդէպ	toward	իր եղբօր հանդէպ	toward his brother.

103

նման, պէս	like	իր մօրը նման	like his mother.
		վարդի մը պէս	like a rose.
մօտ	near	Դուռին մօտ	near the door.
դէմ	against	Այդ մարդուն դէմ	against that man.

c. Accusative:

ի վեր	up the	Բլուրն ի վեր	up the hill.
ի վար	down the	Գետն ի վար	down the river.

d. Ablative:

առաջ	before	ճաշէն առաջ	before dinner
ետք, յետոյ		ճաշէն ետք	after dinner
վերջ	after	տարիէ մը վերջ	one year later
դուրս	out	տունէն դուրս ելայ	I went out of the house
ներս	into, inside of	սենեակէն ներս մտայ	I went into the room
վեր	up	սանդուխէն վեր վազեցի	I ran up the stairs
վար	down	պատէն վար ցատկեցի	I jumped down from the wall
դատ	beside, excepting	քեզմէ դատ ամէն ոք Հայերէն խօսեցաւ	excepting you everybody spoke Armenian
սկսեալ	beginning	վաղուընէ սկսեալ	beginning with to-morrow
իվեր	since	անցեալ ամիսէն ի վեր	since last month
ասդին	this side	գետէն ասդին	this side of the river
անդին	that side, beyond	պատէն անդին	the other side of, beyond the wall
Հեռու	far	մարդերէ Հեռու	far from men

e. Instrumental:

Հանդերձ	with	բարեկամներով Հանդերձ	together with friends

104

Note: A few of these prepositions may be placed both before and after the noun:

հանդէպ *եղբօրը* or *եղբօրը* հանդէպ — Toward his brother

բաղդատմամբ *քրոջը* or *քրոջը* բաղդատմամբ — Compared with his sister

Exercise: (On Prepositions)

Չե՞ր եղբայրէն առա՞ջ եկաք — Did you come before your brother?

Ո՛չ, եղբայրէս ետք եկայ — No. I came after my brother.

Կարելի չէ ապրիլ առանց օդի — It is not possible to live without air.

Թատրոն գնաց փոխանակ դպրոց երթալու — He went to the theater instead of going to school.

Դէպի քաղաք գացին — They went toward the city.

Մինչեւ վաղը պիտի սպասենք — We shall wait until tomorrow.

Մինչեւ առաւօտ չքնացայ — I did not sleep until morning.

Մինչեւ դպրոց միասին քալեցինք — We walked together as far as the school.

Հակառակ խրատիս՝ մեկնեցաւ — Contrary to my advice, he left.

Բացի ձեր եղբայրէն բոլոր ընկերներս հոս են — Except your brother all my companions are here.

Հակառակ ջանքերուս ձախողեցայ — In spite of my efforts I failed.

Եղբայրը բարկացած է քրոջը դէմ — The brother is angry against his sister.

Սեղանին վրայ դրիրքեր դրի — I placed books on the table.

Դաշտ մը կայ մեր տունին դիմաց — There is a field opposite our house.

Պատ մը կայ պարտէզին շուրջ — There is a wall around the garden.

Այս նիւթին մասին խօսեցայ — I spoke about this subject.

Քաջ է եղբօրը նման — He is brave like his brother.

Նոյնքան քաջ է որքան իր եղբայրը — He is as brave as his brother.

Չեր քոյրէն ետք եկաւ | He came after your sister.

Չեզմէ առաջ Հայերէն պիտի սորվիմ | I shall learn Armenian before you.

Կ՚ուզէ՞ք խաղալ ինծի հետ | Do you want to play with me?

Գրիչ մը կ՚ուզեմ եղբօրս համար | I want a pen for my brother.

Լեզու կը սորվիմ խօսելու համար | I learn (a) language in order to speak.

Այս օրէն սկսեալ | Beginning with today.

Այս առաւօտէն սկսեալ | Beginning with this morning.

Ամէն օր թերթ մը պիտի ղրկեմ | I shall send a newspaper every day.

Քաղաքէն անդին դաշտ մը կայ | There is a field beyond the city.

12

Adverbs — ՄԱԿԲԱՑՆԵՐ

Adverbs are invariable words modifying verbs, adjectives or other adverbs:

շատ սիրել to love much   քիչ խոսիլ to speak little

Adverbs may signify:

a. Place:

հոս	here	ներս	in, into, inside	մօտ	near
հոն	there	դուրս	out, outside	վեր	up
ուր	where	հեռու	far	վար	down

b. Quantity:

շատ	much	բաւական	enough		
նուազ	little	չափազանց	too much	ամենէն շատ	at most
քիչ	more	գրեթէ	almost	առ առաւելն	
աւելի	less	առնուազն	at least		

c. Time:

կանուխ	early	հազիւ	hardly	մխանդամ ընդ միշտ	once for all
հիմա	now	նախ	at first		
ուշ	late	երբեմն	sometimes		
այսօր	today	յետոյ	afterward		
երէկ	yesterday	երբ	when		

107

վաղը	tomorrow	առ այժմ	for the time being
միշտ	always	յանկարծ	suddenly
յաճախ	often	օրէ օր	day by day
առներոք	formerly	աւելի եւս	hereafter
		այսուհետեւ	

d. Affirmation, denial, doubt:

այո	yes	բնաւ, երբեք	never
ոչ	no	թերեւս	perhaps
ամենեւին	not at all	իրաւ	truly
անշուշտ	of course	արդարեւ	in fact
ապահովապար	surely	հաւանորէն	probably
		զուր, ի զուր	in vain

e. Manner:

ինչպէս	how	դանդաղորէն	slowly
մեծապէս	greatly	ընդհանրապէս	generally
այսպէս	so, thus	կամաւ	willingly
արագօրէն	quickly	ակամայ	unwillingly

Besides single words, there are adverbial locutions:

տեղ տեղ	here and there	մէկիկ մէկիկ	one by one
քովէ քով	side by side	փոխն ի փոխ	alternately
մէկէն ի մէկ	all at once	մաս մաս	in parts

Adverbs may be formed by affixing certain particles like:
աբար, օրէն, ապէս, ովին, to nouns, adjectives and verbal roots:

Examples

հայր+աբար – հայրաբար	in a fatherly manner, paternally
խոնարհ+աբար – խոնարհաբար	humbly
անկեղծ+օրէն անկեղծօրէն	sincerely
յաւերժ+օրէն – յաւերժօրէն	eternally
վեհանձն+օրէն վեհանձնօրէն	generously
ազգ+ովին – ազգովին	nationally
պարզ+ապէս – պարզապէս	simply

108

ընդհանուր+ապէս – ընդհանրապէս	generally
մանաւոր+ապէս մանաւորապէս	specially
բոլոր+ովին – բոլորովին	altogether
հիմն+ովին – հիմնովին	basically

Exercise

Հոս եկէք	Come here.
Երբեք մի' ստէք	Never tell lies.
Հազիւ կրնայ կարդալ	He can hardly read.
Թերեւս լսեցիք թէ Հայերէն կը սորվիմ	Perhaps you heard that I am learning Armenian.
Եթէ կամաւ չերթաս, բռնի կը տանին քեզ	If you do not go willingly they carry you by force.
Ի՞նչպէս կ'ուզէք որ կարդամ	How do you want me to read?
Աւելի կամաց կարդա'	Read more slowly.
Քիչ խօսիլ, շատ խորհիլ	To speak little, to think much.
Նախ դուրս ելան, յետոյ ներս եկան	They first went out, then they came in.
Տղաք անշուշտ կը սիրեն իրենց ծնողքը	Children of course love their parents.
Մեծապէս կը գնահատեմ	I greatly appreciate.
Խորապէս երախտապարտ եմ	I am deeply grateful.
Այս մարդը առնուազն յիսուն տարեկան է	This man is at least fifty years old.
Մարդիկ ընդհանրապէս եսասէր են	Men are generally selfish.
Երբ ձմեռը գայ, գարունը կրնա՞յ շատ հեռու ըլլալ	When winter comes, can spring be far behind?

CONJUNCTIONS – ՇԱՂԿԱՊՆԵՐ

These are invariable words which join words, clauses and sentences. The principal ones are the following:

ու, եւ	and	բայց	but
նաեւ, ալ	also	այսինքն	that is to say
այլ նաեւ	but also	թէեւ, թէպէտեւ	though, although
անգամ, նոյն իսկ	even	այնպէս որ	so that

109

կամ	or	*միայն*	only
կա'մ... կա'մ...	either... or...	*մինչ*	while
ո'չ... ոչ...	neither... nor...	*պայմանով որ*	provided
թէ'... թէ...	both... and...	*ուրեմն, ուստի*	therefore
քանի... այնքան աւելի	the more... the more...		
որ	that	*քանի որ*	since
եթէ	if	*վասն զի*	for, because
ո'չ թէ... այլ	not that... but	*որպէս զի*	in order that
որովհետեւ, ինչու որ	because		
ո'չ որովհետեւ... այլ որովհետեւ *ո'չ որովհետեւ... այլ այն* *պատճառով որ*	not because ... but because		
ո'չ միայն... այլ նաեւ	not only... but also		

Exercise

Կատուն ու շունը ընտանի կենդանիներ են	The cat and the dog are domestic animals.
Քոյրս եւ ես կը սիրենք կարդալ	My sister and I love to read.
Կա'մ կը խօսի, կա'մ կը գրէ	He either speaks or writes.
Կը փափաքիմ որ դուն ալ գաս	I wish that you also come.
Թէ' պիտի խօսիմ, թէ' պիտի երգեմ	I shall both speak and sing.
Պիտի սորվիք, պայմանով որ աշխատիք	You will learn provided you work.
Մինչ դուք կուգայիք, ես կ'երթայի	While you were coming I was going.
Պիտի չերթամ քանի որ դուք հոն պիտի չըլլաք	I shall not go since you will not be there.
Ո'չ միայն կը կարդամ այլ նաեւ կը գրեմ	Not only do I read but I also write.
Ո'չ որովհետեւ օրէնքը կը սիրեն, այլ որովհետեւ օրէնքէն կը վախնան	Not because they love the law but because they are afraid of the law.
Այս գիրքը կամ այդ գիրքը	This book or that book.
Պիտի երթամ որովհետեւ խոստացայ	I shall go because I promised.

110

Աշխատէ՛ որպէս զի սորվիս — Work in order that you learn.

Պիտի սերտեմ մինչեւ որ սորվիմ, մինչդեռ դուն պիտի խաղաս — I shall study until I learn, while you will be playing.

Եթէ դուք երթաք, ես ալ ձեզի հետ կ՚երթամ — If you go I also shall go with you.

Մանաւանդ որ ես ալ կը սիրեմ մեր մայրաքաղաքը — Especially as I also love our capital.

Ե՛ս անգամ զարմացայ — Even I was surprised.

Նոյնիսկ բարեկամներս դժուարաւ հաւատացին — Even my friends believed with difficulty.

Անկողին պիտի երթամ որովհետեւ յոգնած եմ — I shall go to bed because I am tired.

Ո՛չ պիտի կարդամ, ո՛չ պիտի գրեմ — I shall neither read nor write.

Բայց այդ պատիժ է, ո՛չ թէ հանգիստ — But that is punishment not rest.

«Նո՛յն իսկ իմ ես՝ ազատատութիւնս հառաչով մ՚ը վերստացայ» — "Even I regained my freedom with a sigh."— (Prisoner of Chillon-Byron)

INTERJECTIONS - ՁԱՅՆԱՐԿՈՒԹԻՒՆՆԵՐ

These are invariable words expressing sudden feelings such as surprise, pain, regret, joy etc.

ո՛հ, ա՛հ   oh! ah! express joy, yearning

ա՛խ, վա՛խ, վա՛յ   express pain, regret woe!

աւա՛ղ, ափսո՛ս   alas!

երանի՛ թէ   would that!

կեցցէ՛   long live!

կեցի՛ս
ապրի՛ս   bravo!

մե՛ղք   what a pity!

անէ՛ծք   malediction!

Examples

Ո՛հ ինչ անո՛ւշ   Oh! How sweet . . .

Մե՛ղք, հազա՛ր մեղք   Pity, a thousand times pity!

Վա՛յ ձեզի կեղծաւորնե՛ր   Woe unto you, hypocrites!

Կեցցե՛ս, լաւ խոսեցար   Bravo, you spoke well!

Երանի՛ ձեզի   Happy are you . . .

111

IDIOMS

խորհիլ, խօսիլ ն‿ի‿թ‿ի մ‿ը մասին   To think, to speak **about** some
  կ‿ա‿մ վրայ   one, something.

ըսել ուզել   to mean.   ի°ն‿չ ըսել կ'ուզէք   what do you mean?

առիթով, առթիւ   on the occasion of

պատճառով   because of

Հաճեցէ'ք   Please!

եթէ կը Հաճիք   if you please.

Կը Հաճի°ք   will you please?

Մ‿ի‿ս‿ կողմէ   on the other hand.

Օրինակի Համար, զոր օրինակ,   for example.

որոշում առալ,   to make a decision.

Տեղի ունենալ   to take place,   տեղի տալ   to yield

Հաճոյքով, սիրով   with pleasure.

Շնորհակալ եմ   Thank you!

Ո'արժեր, խնդրեմ   Welcome! Nothing! Please!

Դպրոցը պիտի մնամ   I shall stay at the school.

Տունը   ”   ”   I shall stay at home.
                                      (In Armenian no preposition is
                                      required in this instance.)

Դպրոց պիտի երթամ   I shall go (to) school. (The pre-
                                      position **to**, dative case, not
                                      needed in Armenian.)

Քաղաք   ”   ”   I shall go (to) town.

Լոնտոն   ”   ”   I shall go (to) London.

Վստահ եմ թէ   I am sure that . . .

Լաւ ատեն անցնել   To have a fine time.

Մ‿ե'ղք որ   It is a pity that . . .

Այսինքն   That is to say

Այնպէս չէ°   Isn't it so?

Շատոնց է որ   It is a long time since . . .

Ուրախ եմ (որ եկաք)   I am glad that . . . (you came.)

Կը ցաւիմ որ (չկրցաք գալ)   I am sorry that . . . (you could
                                      not come.)

Միջոցներ ձեռք առնել   To take measures.

112

13

Derivative and Compound Words
Suppression and Permutation of Vowels
Formation of New Words With Old Ones

Words are of three kinds:

1. ROOTS, when they are in their simple form without any addition:

   ազգ   nation   ձայն   voice   արժէք   value

2. DERIVED, when a particle is added to a Root, as prefix or suffix:

   ազգ+ային = ազգային   national
   ձայն+ական = ձայնական   vocal
   ան+արժէք = անարժէք   valueless, worthless
   Հայ+աստան = Հայաստան   Armenia

3. COMPOUND words, formed by the union of two or more words, giving rise to a new word having a new meaning:

   ծով+եզերք = ծովեզերք   seashore
   մարտ+ա+նաւ = մարտանաւ   battleship

   In forming derivative or compound words, and in declensions and conjugations, vowels and diphthongs in the last syllables of words undergo certain changes: they may be dropped entirely or changed to a different vowel:

113

a. The letters *ի* and *ու* are generally dropped entirely:

սիրտ (heart) *սրտագին* (hearty). *գիր* – *գրական* (literary)
գույթ (pity) *գթասիրտ* (charitable). *սուտ* – *ստախոս* (liar)

b. The letter *է* is changed to *ի*:

սէր – *սիրելի* (dear)

c. The diphthong *եա* is changed to *ե*:

մատեան (book), *մատենագիր* (author)

d. The diphthong *ոյ* is changed to *ու*:

լոյս – *լուսաւոր* (luminous). *գոյն* – *գունաւոր* (colored)

e. The diphthong *իւ* is changed to *ու*:

պատիւ (honor). *պատուաւոր* (honorable)

f. The diphthong *եայ* is changed to *է*:

քրիստոնեայ (Christian, noun). *քրիստոնէական*
(Christian, adj.)

Հրեայ (Jew, noun). *Հրէական* (Jewish, adj.)

DERIVATIVE WORDS: ԱԾԱՆՑ ԲԱՌԵՐ

1. Formed by Prefixes such as:

   ան, ապ, տ, չ, դժ, տժ.— give a negative meaning:

արժան	worthy	*անարժան*	unworthy
օրէնք	law	*ապօրէն*	unlawful
գոյն	color	*տժգոյն*	pale, colorless
գէտ (*գիտնալ*)	know	*տգէտ*	ignorant
բախտ	luck	*դժբախտ*	unlucky, unfortunate, unhappy

   անդր – beyond

   անդրաշխարհ   the world beyond
   անդրշիրիմեան   beyond the grave

   գեր – idea of superiority

գերմարդ superman   *գերիշխան* suzerain

   ստոր – under

ստորագծել underline   *ստորերկրեայ* underground

114

վեր   again   վերստանալ   to get back

2. Formed by Suffixes such as:

ապար, օրէն — these suffixes form adverbs:

խոնարհ	humble	խոնարհապար	humbly
մեղմ	mild	մեղմօրէն	mildly
փափուկ	delicate	փափկօրէն	delicately

ալի, ելի — form adjectives:

ցաւալի	painful	սքանչելի	wonderful
ողբալի	mournful	հրաշալի	marvelous
շնորհալի	graceful	հաճելի	agreeable

ակ, իկ, ուկ — these are diminutive suffixes.

գետ	river	գետակ	small river, stream
նաւ	boat	նաւակ	small, rowing boat

ական — forms adjectives: օգտական, վնասական   useful, harmful.

ական, ային: form adjectives with a meaning of belonging:

ազգ	nation	ազգային	national
հրեշտակ	angel	հրեշտակային	angelic
հայկական	Armenian	անգլիական	English
ձայն	voice	ձայնական	vocal
հայր	father	հայրական	fatherly

անոց, նոց — indicating place for:

հիւանդ	sick	հիւանդանոց	hospital
զօրք	soldier	զօրանոց	barracks

արէն, երէն — give the meaning of language.

յունարէն	Greek language	հայերէն	Armenian
չինարէն	Chinese	ֆրանսերէն	French
անգլերէն	English	ռուսերէն	Russian

արան — idea of place

    restaurant, dining-room   ճաշարան

    ընթերցարան, վառարան, լսարան

ացի – denoting origin

Ամերիկացի	(an) American	*Անգլիացի*	Englishman
Ֆրանսացի	Frenchman	*Ճապոնցի*	Japanese

աւոր – forms adjectives and nouns

փառք	glory	*փառաւոր*	glorious
սուգ	mourning	*սգաւոր*	mourner
վէրք	wound	*վիրաւոր*	wounded (adj.)

եղէն – gives the meaning of **made of**:

ոսկի	gold	*ոսկեղէն*	golden
հուր	fire	*հրեղէն*	made of fire
արծաթ	silver	*արծաթեղէն*	of silver
բուրդ	wool	*բրդեղէն*	woolen

ենի – added to name of fruit, gives the word for the tree:

խնձոր, խնձորենի	apple tree
թուղ, թղենի	fig tree
նարինջ, նարնջենի	orange tree
տանձ, տանձենի	pear tree

ական – forms adjectives: *արեւմտական*, western

ոտ – forms adjectives from nouns:

ջուր	water	*ջրոտ*	watery	*ադտ*	dirt	*ադտոտ*	dirty

ուհի – forms feminine nouns:

դերասան actor		*դերասանուհի*	actress
Հայ Armenian		*Հայուհի*	Armenian girl or woman
սուրբ saint		*սրբուհի*	woman saint

ուտ – forms adjectives:

տիղմ mud		*տղմուտ* muddy		*աւազուտ* sandy

որդ, պան, իչ – form nouns denoting agents:

որս	prey	*որսորդ*	hunter
պարտէզ	garden	*պարտիզպան*	gardener
նաւ	boat	*նաւորդ*	navigator
հաւաքել	collect	*հաւաքիչ*	collector
դիւթ(el)	enchant	*դիւթիչ*	enchanting

ութիւն, ում, ոյք, ուածք, անք – form nouns denoting action or condition:

բարի, *բարութիւն*	goodness
չար, *չարութիւն*	badness
մանուկ child *մանկութիւն*	childhood
հաւաք(ել), *հաւաքոյք*	gathering
հալած(ել), *հալածանք*	persecution
շէն(ք), *շինուածք*	construction

պէս – forms adverbs:

մեծ, *մեծապէս*	greatly
յայտնի, *յայտնապէս*	evidently
մասնաւորապէս	specially

ովին – gives the idea of togetherness

բոլորովին	altogether
ազգովին	the whole nation in unison
խմբովին	as a group

COMPOUND WORDS: ԲԱՐԴ ԲԱՌԵՐ

Compound words are formed by joining:

1. Noun to noun: *սեղան+ա+տուն* = dining-room.
2. Noun to a verbal root: *կառ(ք)+ա+վար(ել)* = *կառավար* = driver, coachman.
3. Adjective to a noun: *թանկ+արժէք* = precious.
4. Preposition or adverb to a noun: *նախ+ա+դուռ* = antechamber.
5. Preposition or adverb to a verbal root: *վեր+ելք* = rise.
6. Pronoun to a verbal root: *ինքն+ա+շարժ* = automobile.

The joining of the words is made:

a. simply by putting them next to each other:
   ծով+եզերք – *ծովեզերք* = seashore
   կէս (half) + *օր* – *կէսօր* = noon

b. by joining the two words with the letter ա

բարձր (high) + ա + ձայն = բարձրաձայն   aloud

մարտ (battle) + ա + նաւ = մարտանաւ   battleship

If the first word ends in the vowel ի, the letter ե is used as adjoiner instead of ա, and the vowel ի is dropped:

գինի (wine) + ե + տուն = գինետուն   saloon

շոգի (steam) + ե + նաւ = շոգենաւ   steamer

c. by joining them with the letters եւ or ու:

առ + եւ + տուր = առեւտուր   trade (give and take)

ահ (fear) + ու + դող = ահուդող   terror

Exercise

A. Separate the following compound and derivative words:

ոսկեդար – ոսկի + դար = golden age

հիւրանոց – հիւր + անոց = guest room, inn

գրատուն – գիրք (ք) + տուն = library

գարեջուր – գարի + ջուր = beer

անչափ – ան (prefix) + չափ = immeasurable

անօգուտ – ան + օգուտ = useless

ցեխոտ – ցեխ + ոտ (suffix) = muddy

դասարան – դաս + արան = classroom

կիսամերկ – կէս + մերկ = half naked

կիսաստուած – կէս + աստուած = demigod

լայնութիւն – լայն + ութիւն (suf.) = width

անմահ – ան (pref.) + մահ = immortal

նիստուկաց – նիստ + կաց = behavior

արեւոտ – արեւ + ոտ (suf.) = sunny

ինքնահաւան – ինքն + հաւան = pretentious

եսասէր – ես + սէր = selfish

կերուխում – կեր + խում = drink

յառաջաբան – յառաջ + բան (word) = foreword, preface

մեղրահամ – մեղր + համ (taste) = tasting like honey

մշտատեւ – միշտ + տեւ (ել) (to last) = everlasting

դիւրավառ – դիւր (easy) + վառ (burn) = inflammable

շահաւոր – շահ + աւոր (suf.) = profitable

118

B. Form compound words with the following words:

դեկ, վար(ել) – դեկավար	helmsman, leader
բազուկ, աթոռ – բազկաթոռ	armchair
երկինք, կամար – երկնակամար	sky
նախ, քայլ – նախաքայլ	preliminary step
վերջ, լույս – վերջալույս	sunset
երկիր, շարժ – երկրաշարժ	earthquake
արեւ, ելք – արեւելք	east
արեւ, մուտք – արեւմուտք	west
կառք, խումբ – կառախումբ	train
տուն, տիկին – տանտիկին	housewife
հայր, եղբայր – հորեղբայր	uncle
ծաղիկ, փունջ – ծաղկեփունջ	bouquet of flowers
լի, լուսին – լիալուսին	full moon
բառ, ցանկ – բառացանկ	vocabulary
շարժ, նկար – շարժանկար	movies

14

Infinitive, Participles, Verbs and Their Cases

INFINITIVE: ԱՆԵՐԵՒՈԹ

The infinitive of verbs may be used as a noun and therefore be declined and take an article. When declined, the infinitives of all three declensions *ել*, *իլ*, *ալ*, follow the pattern of *ծով*, *ծովու*, *ծովէ*, *ծովով*: Thus: *սիրել — սիրելու*, *խօսիլ — խօսելու*, *կարդալ — կար-դալու*:

Examples

Nominative:

Կարդալը հաճոյք է | To read is pleasure.
Սիրելը երջանկութիւն է | To love is happiness.

Accusative:

Կարդալը կը սիրեմ, գրելը ո՛չ այնքան | I like to read, not so much to write.

Genitive:

Նկարելու արուեստը | The art of painting (to paint).
Կարդալու վայելքը | The enjoyment of reading (of to read).

Dative:

Հասկանալու համար	In order to understand (for to understand).
Փոխանակ խաղալու՝ աշխատէ՝	Work instead of playing (to play).

Ablative:

Խորհէ՝ խօսելէ առաջ	Think before speaking!
Սատէ զղուշացէ՝ր	Keep away from lying (from to lie).

Instrumental:

Մտածելով խօսիլ	To speak (with) thinking.
Սիրելով ապրիլ, սիրուելով մեռնիլ	To live loving, to die being loved.

The past infinitive is formed by the participle of the verb and the infinitive of the auxiliary verb: *ըլլալ.—*

Սիրած ըլլալ	to have loved
Խօսած ըլլալ	to have spoken

When declined, the participle remains unchanged, it is the auxiliary that is declined: *սիրած ըլլալով, խօսած ըլլալու համար:*

PARTICIPLES: ԸՆԴՈՒՆԵԼՈՒԹԻՒՆ or ԴԵՐԲԱՅ

Participles function both as verbs and nouns. They can be declined and they take an article. There are three participles:

Present: which ends with: *ող – սիրող* (loving)
Past: which ends with: *ած, եր – սիրած, սիրեր* (loved)
Future: which ends with: *լու, լիք – սիրելու, սիրելիք*

Participles ending in *եր* and *լու* are not used as nouns. They only form the compound tenses with the auxiliary verb *ըլլալ* as we saw previously: *սիրած եմ, սիրած էի, սիրած պիտի ըլլամ, սիրելու եմ*, etc.

The participles ending in *ող, ած, լու* and *լիք,* are also used as adjectives:

գործող միտք	acting mind
աւարտած գործ	completed task
եփելու ջուր	water to be boiled
կարդալիք գիրք	book to be read

As nouns:

Աշխատողը կը յաջողի	The working (man) succeeds.
Պատի՛ւ աշխատողին	Honor to the working (man).

Participles used adjectively imply a relative pronoun. Thus: *եկող մարդը* (the coming man) means: the man **who** comes. *եկած մարդը* means the "man who came." It is very common that instead of the relative pronoun, the participle form is used as follows:

Instead of saying:

Մարդը որ կուգայ հայրս է (the man who is coming is my father),

we can say: *Եկող մարդը հայրս է:*

Տունը որ ես կը տեսնեմ մեծ է The house which I see is big.

This can be rendered also without the relative pronoun (*որ*) as follows:

իմ տեսած տունս մեծ է:

It is apparent that this construction is obtained by putting the subject of the verb (*ես*, in this instance) in the genitive case *իմ*, and using the past participle of the verb, adding to the direct object the possessive article of the subject, *ս* in this case.

Likewise, instead of saying:

Տունը որ դուն կը տեսնես մեծ է,	we can say:
Քու տեսած տունդ մեծ է	In the same way:
Անոր տեսած տունը մեծ է	The house he sees is big (or he saw).
Մեր տեսած տունը մեծ է	The house we see is big (we saw).
Ձեր տեսած տունը մեծ է	The house you see is big (you saw).
Անոնց տեսած տունը մեծ է	The house they see is big (or they saw).
Անոնց տեսած տունը մեծ էր	The house they saw was big.

122

The noun in this construction can also be declined:

Քու տեսած տունէդ կուգամ	I come from the house which you saw.
Քեր տեսած տունին դուռը	The door of the house which you saw.
Անոնց կարդացած գիրքին անունը	The name of the book which they read.

The Future Participles *լու* and *լիք* give a meaning of obligation in futurity.

լու is used to form compound tenses with the auxiliary *ըլլալ*:—

երթալու եմ	I must go
տեսնելու եմ	I must see
տեսնուելու եմ	I must be seen
յարգուելու ես	You should be respected
դասդ սորվելու ես	You must learn your lesson

լիք is not used to form compound tenses it is used adjectively and also gives a meaning of obligation:

Թափուելիք ջուր	Water to be thrown away.
Տեսնելիք մարդս դեռ չէ եկած	The man whom I must see has not yet come.
Երթալիք տեղս հեռու է	The place where I have to go is far.

VOCABULARY

կառավարութիւն	government	*ծովակալ*	admiral
խորհրդարան	parliament	*ծերակոյտ*	senate
սահմանադրութիւն	constitution	*ծերակուտական*	senator
օրէնք	law	*հողային*	territorial
արդարութիւն	justice	*անկախութիւն*	indepen-dence
հաւասարութիւն	equality		
հանրապետութիւն	republic	*վարչութիւն*	adminis-tration
հանրապետական	republican		
ժողովրդավարութիւն	democracy	*առաջնորդ*	leader
ժողովրդավար	democrat	*քաղաքականութիւն*	politics
նախագահ	president	*քաղաքական*	political

123

փոխ–նախախագահ	vice-president	քաղաքապետ	mayor
երեսփոխան	deputy, congressman	օրէնսդիր	legislative
դահլիճ	cabinet	գործադիր	executive
նախարար	minister, secretary	դատական	judicial
իշխանութիւն	authority	դատարան	court, tribunal
բանակ	army	դատաւոր	judge
նաւատորմիղ	navy	փաստաբան	lawyer
զօրավար	general	ընտրութիւն	election
		քուէարկել	to vote
		կուսակցութիւն	party
		կառավարիչ	governor

Exercise

Մեր երկիրը Հանրապետու–թիւն մըն է	Our country is a republic.
Սահմանադրութիւնը անոր Հիմնական օրէնքն է	The Constitution is its fundamental law.
Ան կը կառավարուի օրէնքներով	It is governed by laws.
Ժողովուրդը կ'ընտրէ իր առաջ–նորդները	The people elects its leaders.
Իր ընտրած երեսփոխանները ու ծերակուտականները օրէնս–դիրներն են։	The deputies (congressmen) and the senators whom they elect are the legislators. (With past participle instead of relative pronoun).
Երեսփոխանները ու ծերակու–տականները զորս ան կ'ընտրէ օրէնսդիրներն են։	Same as the preceding; different construction (with relative pronoun).
Ժողովուրդը օրէնքները յար–գելու է	The people must respect the laws.
Խounդը (noun) նախագահն է	**The person who is speaking is the President.**
Խounդ (adj.) անձը նախագահն է	The **speaking** person is the President.

Ընտրուելիք կառավարիչը կա— | The Governor to be elected must
րող անձ մը ըլլալու է | be a capable person.

Ճարդուած մէկու մը ընտրուիլը | The election ("the being elect-
խիստ հաւանական է | ed," infin.) of a respected
| person is most probable.

Սխալիլը մարդկային է, ներելը | To err is human, to forgive di-
աստուածային | vine.

Verbs Requiring Dative Case

Certain transitive verbs which in English take the accusative case, require the dative in Armenian:

հաւատալ	believe	ներել	pardon, forgive
վստահիլ	trust	խնայել	spare
նպաստել	favor, con-	նախանձիլ	envy
	tribute	ձգտիլ	tend
օգնել	help	նայիլ	look
սպառնալ	threaten	նմանիլ	resemble
սպասել	wait	մօտենալ	approach
հնազանդիլ	obey	յաղթել	conquer
հրամայել	command	վնասել	harm
հետեւիլ	follow	ծառայել	serve
հանդիպիլ	meet	ունկնդրել	listen to
ցանկալ, տենչ—	yearn	տիրանալ	become the
չալ			owner of
աղաչել	beg, entreat	տիրել	rule, reign

Examples

Կը հաւատամ ձեզի | I believe (to) you.
Իր խօսքին հաւատացի | I believed (to) his word.
Հետեւեցէք ինծի | Follow (to) me.
Պիտի սպասեմ բարեկամիս | I shall wait (to) for my friend.
Ան սպառնաց ինծի | He threatened (to) me.
Դատի մը ծառայել | To serve (to) a cause.
Ներեցէք ինծի | Pardon (to) me.

125

Մի՛ մօտենաք կրակին	Do not approach (to) the fire.
Շատեր կը նախանձին ձեզի	Many people envy (to) you.
Երէկ ձեր եղբօրը հանդիպեցայ	I met (to) your brother yesterday.
Օգնէ՛ ընկերիդ	Help (to) your friend.
Վստահեցայ իրեն եւ յուսա-խաբ չեղայ	I trusted him and I was not disappointed.
Ալքոլը կը վնասէ առողջութեան	Alcohol is harmful to health.
Նայեցէ՛ք ասա մարդուն	Look (to) at this man.
Աշխատութեամբ կը յաղթենք դժուարութեանց	We overcome (to) difficulties by work.
Հաճոյքով ունկնդրեցի իր ուղերձին	I listened with pleasure to his discourse.

Adjectives Requiring Dative

These denote nearness, likeness, fitness:

նման	like	պատրաստ	ready
յարմար	fit	հաւասար	equal
վնասակար	harmful	կարող	able
օգտակար	useful	հաճելի	agreeable
սիրելի	dear	կարօտ	needy
արժանի	worthy	ծարաւի	thirsty

Examples

Մեկնելու պատրաստ եմ	I am ready to leave.
Պատիւներու արժանի էք	You are worthy (to) of honors.
Խախախոտը վնասակար է ձեզի	Tobacco is harmful to you.
Այս քառակուսին հաւասար չէ այդ մ՚իւսին	This square is not equal to that other one.
Այդ երգը հաճելի է ինծի	That song is agreeable to me.
Այդ դերասանները սիրելի են մեզի	Those actors are dear to us.
Այս տունը բնակութեան յարմար չէ	This house is not fit (to) for residence.
Ընտանի կենդանիները մեզի օգտակար են	The domestic animals are useful to us.
Այս տղան իր հօրը նման է	This boy is like his father.

Verbs Requiring Ablative Case

վախնալ	to fear	*հրաժարիլ*	renounce, resign
զրկել	to deprive	*զգուշանալ*	to be careful
փախչիլ	escape	*զզուիլ*	to be disgusted
տառապիլ	suffer	*ձանձրանալ*	to be bored
դադրիլ	cease	*զանիլ, զզուալ*	to loathe
խնդրել	ask, request	*տարբերիլ*	differ
բաղկանալ	consist of		

Adjectives Requiring Ablative Case

զուրկ	deprived of	*դժգոհ*	dissatisfied
զատ	aside from	*զերծ*	free from
տարբեր	different	*ազատ*	free from
գոհ	contented	*հեռու*	far

Verbs Requiring Instrumental Case

զբաղիլ	} to be occupied	*հպարտանալ*	to be proud of (with)
պարապիլ	} with . . .		
բաւականանալ	to be satis-	*պարծենալ*	to boast (with)
գոհանալ	fied with . . .		

Adjectives Requiring Instrumental Case

հարուստ	rich	*լի, լեցուն*	full
ծոխ		*հպարտ*	proud

Exercise

Մի՛ վախնար իրմէ	Don't be afraid (from) of him.
Կրակէ փախչիլ	To escape from fire.
Մխելէ դադրեցայ	I ceased (from) smoking.
Խնդրեցի ձեզմէ	I requested (from) you.
Այդ գիրքը երեք մասէ կը բաղկանայ	That book consists of (from) three parts.
Ձգուեցայ այս գործէն	I got tired (from) of this job.
Ձանձրացայ սպասելէ	I was bored (from) by waiting.
Կը տարբերիմ իրմէ	I differ from him.

127

Մեր վիճակէն գոհ ենք	We are satisfied with our condition.
Ինձմէ զատ ո՛չ ոք կար	There was no one beside (from) me.
Գո՞հ էք ձեր տունէն	Are you satisfied (from) with your house.
Մեր տունը հեռու չէ դպրոցէն	Our house is not far from the school.
Ո՞չ ոք զերծ է թերութիւններէ	No one is free (from) of shortcomings.
Այս սենեակը զուրկ է լոյսէ	This room is deprived (from) of light.
Այս տղան տարբեր է իր եղբայրէն	This boy is different from his brother.
Ի՞նչ գործով կը զբաղիք	What is your business? (literally: With what business are you occupied?)
Ես կը բաւականանամ այս չափով	I am satisfied with this much.
Մի՛ պարծենաք ձեր ունեցածով	Don't boast of what you have.
Հպարտացէ՛ք ձեր բարեկամին յաջողութիւնով	Take pride (with) in your friend's success.
Մեր երկիրը հարուստ է հանքերով, ու նաեւ տաղանդաւոր մարդոցմով	Our country is rich in mines and also (with) in men with talent.
Մեր ծովը լեցուն է ձուկով	Our sea is full of fish.
Ամէն ծնողք հպարտ է իր աշխատասէր զաւակներով	All parents are proud of their diligent children.
Դժգոհ եմ իրմէ	I am dissatisfied with (from) him.

IDIOMS

հոգ ընել բանի մը համար	to worry about something
զարմանալ բանի մը համար	to wonder at
հիանալ մէկու մը վրայ	to admire someone
բարկանալ մէկու մը դէմ	to be angry at somebody
խնդալ մէկու մը վրայ	to ridicule some one

128

իր գործին նայիլ to mind one's business

չափէն աւելի excessive, excessively

ա՛լ կը բաւէ that's enough!

պարապ խօսք nonsense

հաճոյք պատճառել to please

ճամբուն ընթացքին on the way

ողջ առողջ հասնիլ to arrive safely

թեւ թեւի arm in arm

ճամբայ ելլել to start

ձեր կարծիքէն եմ I am of your opinion

կտոր կտոր ընել to tear to pieces

շաբաթէ մը in a week

ամիսէ մը in a month

օրէ մը in a day

դիտմամբ on purpose

չափը անցընել, չափազանցել to exaggerate

չ'արժեր it is not worth while

բերել տալ to order to be brought

կախում ունենալ բանէ մը to depend on something

մէկու մը, բանի մը սիրոյն for the sake of someone, something

առ նուազն at least

առ առաւելն at most

որոշ է թէ it is clear that

յայտնի է թէ it is evident that

կարգը ձերն է it is your turn

կարգը մերն է it is our turn

կարգը իմս է it is my turn

կարգը անոնցն է it is their turn

ձեռք սեղմել to shake hands

բարի ախորժակ good appetite

բարի ճամբորդութիւն bon voyage! Pleasant trip!

ներեցէ՛ք, խնդրեմ Pardon me!

ատպարէզ կարդալ to challenge

129

ժամը ամէն մը once every hour

օրը ամէն մը once a day

երեք ժամը ամէն մը every three hours

այս դեղահատը երկու ժամը take this pill every

    ամէն մը առէք   two hours

ի՞նչ օգուտ what is the use!

ի՞նչ փոյթ what does it matter!

15

The Armenian Sentence

The sentence in its simplest form consists of a subject, attribute or direct object and a verb:

Հայրը (subject) բարի (attribute) է (verb).

Հայրը (subject) որդան (direct object) կը սիրէ (verb).

In these two sentences the three elements are reduced to their simplest expression. Each one of them may consist of several words. For instance, the subject of the first sentence might have been:

«Այս պզտիկ, սիրուն որդուն հայրը բարի է.

The attribute also might have been: «շափագանց բարի ու նոյն ատեն չատ բաշ» է:

Likewise, the verb may consist of a group of words - several verbs with modifying adverbs - but whether they be one word or consist of a group of words, the sentence essentially consists of three parts, and the customary order in which they are arranged is: subject, attribute, verb. In the English sentence the verb comes before the attribute; in Armenian it generally comes last.

However, the Armenian sentence is less rigid. In English there is only one way of saying: "I want to ask you something," and this is it. The equivalent in Armenian: (Ես) բան մը ձեզի հարցնել կ'ուզեմ», may also be rendered as:

Չեզի բան մը կ՚ուզեմ հարցնել
Բան մը ձեզի կ՚ուզեմ հարցնել
Բան մը կ՚ուզեմ հարցնել ձեզի
Բան մը ձեզի հարցնել կ՚ուզեմ
Կ՚ուզեմ ձեզի բան մը հարցնել
Կ՚ուզեմ բան մը հարցնել ձեզի

and all of these would be acceptable and correct. However, in changing around the usual order of words care should be taken not to give way to nonsense:

«Մարդը գիրքը կը կարդայ» (The man reads the book) could not be changed around to read:

«Գիրքը մարդը կը կարդայ» The book would be reading the man, which would be absurd!

The subject of a sentence may be:

1. a noun: Զինը ձերմակ է :
2. an adjective used as a noun: Զարերը միշտ չեն պատմունիր :
3. a pronoun: Դուf չատ կ՚աշխատիք:
4. An infinitive: Կարդալը վայելՔը մըն է :

If there is more than one subject the verb is put in the third person plural: Գրիգոր եւ Սարգիս միասին եկան

If the verb has subjects of different persons, it is put in the person which has priority over the other. The first person (I, we) has priority over the second (you) and the third persons (he, they); and the second person has priority over the third:

Դուն եւ ես կը սիրենք պարել | You and I (we) love to dance.

Ես եւ եղբայրս վաղը պիտի | My brother and I (we) shall leave
մեկնինք | tomorrow.

Դուք ու մենք կը նախընտրենք աշխատիլ | You and we (we) prefer to work.

Մենք եւ անոնք միասին | We and they (we) went together.
գացինք |

In each of the above sentences there is among the subjects a pronoun of first person, therefore the verb is put in the first person plural.

132

Դուն ու Գրիգոր մասին չէք
խաղար

You and Krikor (you) do not play
together.

Դուք ու անոնք ազգական-
ներ էք

You and they (you) are rela-
tives.

The second person (դուն, դուք) having priority over the third
- in these two sentences Krikor and "they" - the verb is put in the
second person plural.

Vocabulary

Հերոս	hero	անմոռանալի	unforgettable
Հզոր	mighty	ընդվզիլ	to revolt
Ջանալ	to try	ազգովին	the whole nation
տիրանալ	to become the lord, the owner of	հակառակ	in spite of
ջնջել	to destroy, wipe out	դիւցազնորէն	heroically
կրօնք	religion	կռուիլ	to fight
կրակապաշ-տութիւն	fire worship	ահեղ	awesome
բռնի	forcibly	բանակ	army
տեղի ունենալ	to take place	պատմական	historic
ընկեր	companion	ճակատամարտ	battle
պատերազմ	war	պարտուիլ	to be defeated
կորսուիլ	to be lost	խիղճ	conscience
համոզուիլ	to be convinced	ազատութիւն	liberty
պատել	to separate	դատ	cause
տեղի տալ	to yield	կարենալ	to be able to
զոհել	to sacrifice	հաւատք	faith
համոզել	to convince	ամէն ինչ	everything
համոզուիլ	to be convinced	կորսնցնել	to lose
երբեք	never	կորսուիլ	to be lost
երախտագի-տութիւն	gratitude	վերջապէս	at last
		մնալ	to remain
Հայրենիք	fatherland	առիւծասիրտ	lion-hearted
		ախոյեան	champion
		նահատակ	martyr

133

TO THE STUDENT

As a conclusion to the preceding chapters we shall give here a few pages of prose which you should be able to translate into English. You will find in them the application of the rules which you learned. If there are any words which you have not already met, you will find their meaning in the vocabulary at the end of this book.

We shall translate together the first of these pieces as an example. You can then do the same with the others by yourself and be convinced that you are on the way to mastering the language.

You should make it a habit to read daily an Armenian newspaper, or a book, to enrich your vocabulary and to see in actual operation the rules you learned.

Do not hesitate to speak for fear of making mistakes. Speak with your parents, your friends, and preferably, if possible, with people who know Armenian well. Constant practice in listening, speaking and reading is the secret of acquiring a language.

ՎԱՐԴԱՆ ՄԱՄԻԿՈՆԵԱՆ

Վարդան Մամիկոնեան Հայերուն ազգային հերոսն է։ Հինգերորդ դարուն` Թագկերտ, Պարսիկներու Հզոր Թագաւորը, ջանաց տիրանալ ո՛չ միայն Հայերու երկիրին` Հայաստանին, այլ նաեւ անոնց Հոգիին։ Ան ուզեց ջնջել քրիստոնէութիւնը Հայերու աշխարհէն, եւ բռնի անոր տեղը դնել Պարսիկներու կրօն-քը` կրակապաշտութիւը։

Հայերը ընդվզեցան ազգովին։ Վարդանի առաջնորդու-թեամբ, Հակառակ իրենց փոքր թիւին, անոնք դիւցազնորէն կռուեցան Պարսիկներու անՀեղ բանակին դէմ։ Աւարայրի պատ-մական ճակատամարտն էր այդ, որ տեղի ունեցաւ 451ին։ Վարդան եւ իր ընկերները — Վարդանանք — ինկան պատերազմի դաշտին վրայ, Հայերը պարտուեցան, բայց խիղճի ազատութեան դատը, որուն Համար գոհած էին ամէն ինչ, չկորսուեցաւ։ Պարսիկները Համոզուեցան վերջապէս թէ երբեք պիտի չկարենան Հայերը դա-տել իրենց Հաւատքէն ու տեղի տուին։ Հայերը մնացին իրենց Հո-գիին ու երախտագիտութեամբ կը յիշեն միշտ քաջ Վարդանը եւ իր ընկերները, իբրեւ Հայրենիքի պաշտպան առիւծասիրտ Հե-րոսներ, եւ քրիստոնէութեան ախոյեան` անմոռանալի նաՀա-տակներ։

134

Translation (Sentence by sentence).

1. Vartan Mamigonian is the national hero of the Armenians.

   (Հայերուն - of the Armenians; genitive, plural, of Հայ.
   (ազգային - national; adjective formed with the noun ազգ
   and the suffix ային.

2. In the fifth century, Yazdegerd, the powerful king of the
   Persians, tried to be lord of not only the country of the Armenians but also of their soul.

   (Հինգերորդ - fifth; ordinal adjective formed by the cardinal
   հինգ and the suffix երորդ.

   (դարուն - of the century; genit. of դար, declined like ծով –
   ծովու.

   (ջանաց - he tried; Indicative Perfect of ջանալ, conjugated
   like կարդալ, third conjugation.

   (տիրանալ - to be lord, owner of: takes the dative, therefore երկիրին:

   (ո՛չ միայն... այլ նաեւ - not only... but also; noted in
   the Chapter on Conjunctions.

3. He wanted to wipe out Christianity from the world of the Armenians and put by force in its place the religion of the
   Persians: fire worship.

   (ուզեց - he wanted; perfect of ուզել, verb, first conjugation.

   (ջնջել - to wipe out, first conjug. takes the ablative; hence,
   աշխարհէն:

   (անոր տեղը դնել - to put in its place.

4. The entire Armenian nation revolted. Under the leadership of
   Vartan, in spite of their small number, they fought heroically
   against the mighty army of the Persians.

   (ազգովին - the entire nation; adverb formed with the noun
   ազգ and the suffix ովին:

   (ընդվզեցան - revolted, indic. perfect of ընդվզիլ, verb of
   the second conjugation.

135

($wnw2Gnpryniptwdp$ - with the leadership; instrum. case
of $wnw2Gnpryniptih$:

(ptd - against; postposition; takes dative; hence, $pwGwlhG$
ptd:

5. That was the historic battle of Avarayr which took place in 451.
($wtnh ntGtgwL$ - took place; perf. of $ntGtGwl$:

6. Vartan and his companions - Vartanank - fell on the field of
war, the Armenians were defeated but the cause of the
liberty of conscience, for which they had sacrificed every-
thing, was not lost.
($pGlwG$ - (they) fell; perfect of the irreg. verb $pjGwl$, in
plural because the subject is in plural.

($npniG $wdwp$ - for which; $npniG$ dative of np which is in
the dative with $$wdwp$.

qnwd$ tpG - had sacrificed; compound past perfect of
qntl$:

7. The Persians were convinced at last that they would never be
able to separate the Armenians from their faith and yielded.
($wpipp $twptGwG$ - future present of $twptGwl$ negative
of verb $twptGwl$:

($qwwtl$ - separate; takes the ablative case; hence, $$w-
Lwwptfi$:

($wtnh $wntpG$ - yielded; indic. perfect of irreg. verb wwl:

8. The Armenians remained the masters of their soul and always
remembered with gratitude the Brave Vartan and his companions, as lion-hearted heroes, protectors of their father-
land, and unforgettable martyrs, champions of Christianity.
(wtp - lord, master, owner; takes the genitive: $$nphG$:

($tpwfuwwqfuwntptwdp$ - with gratitude; instrum. case of
$tpwfuwwqfuwntptiG$:

($wnhdwfpwn$ - lion-hearted; compound noun formed with
$wnhd$ and $uppwn$:

ՍՈՒՐԲ ԳՐԻԳՈՐ ԼՈՒՍԱՎՈՐԻՉ

Պատկառելի անձնաւորութիւն մը որ Հայ ազգին ճակատա-
գրին վրայ ամենախոր ազդեցութիւն գործած է։ Թաղթոս եւ
Բարթողոմէոս առաքեալներով Հայաստան բերուած քրիստոնէութիւնը, իրմով վերջնականապէս հաստատուեցաւ Հայոց աշ-
խարհին մէջ երրորդ դարուն։ Ինք եղած է Հայ եկեղեցիին
հիմնադիրն ու առաջին կազմակերպիչը։ Իր տեսիլքով «աշխարհի
լոյսը» Հայոց մէջ փայլեցաւ մշտնջենապէս։ Հայոց թագաւորը՝
Տրդատ, Հռոմի մէջ մեծցած ու կրթուած, կռապաշտ մըն էր,
քրիստոնէայ կոյսեր նահատակելու չափ անդուժ ու մոլեռանդ,
որ դարձի եկաւ խղճմտաբար, եւ կատարեալ զօրծակից մը եղաւ
Գրիգորի այնուհետեւ։

Գրիգոր եղաւ Թբրիստոսի առաքեալ մը։ Ան շրջեցաւ Հա-
յաստանի զանազան գաւառները, Ձնջեց հեթանոսութիւնը, քան-
դեց կռատունները, հինեց եկեղեցիներ, որոնց կարեւորագոյնն
է էջմիածնայ կաթողիկէն, որ կը մնայ անկէ ի վեր Հայոց հո-
գեւոր միութեան կեդրոնը եւ ամենայն Հայոց Հայրապետու-
թեան աթոռը։ Ան պատրաստեց կղերականներ, հիմնեց դպրոց-
ներ, Հասցուց աշակերտներ որոնք կալ պահեցին Արեւմուտքի
լուսաւոր կեդրոններուն հետ, եւ Հայաստան մնաց քրիստոնեայ
քաղաքակրթութեան եւ Արեւմուտքի մշակոյթին նուիրուած՝
անդրդուելիօրէն։

Գրիգոր կոչուեցաւ Լուսաւորիչ ու եղաւ Հայոց ազգային
սուրբը։ Ան անցած է նաեւ Թբրիստոսի տիեզերական եկեղեցուն
սուրբերու դասը ու կը յարգուի օտար քրիստոնեայ եկեղեցինե-
րէն ալ Հաւասարապէս։

137

ՍՈՒՐԲ ՄԵՍՐՈՊ ՄԱՇՏՈՑ

Ուրիշ հակայ մը հանձարեղ, որուն ազդեցութիւնն ալ հայ ազդին ձակատագրին վրայ եղած է խոր ու անշշելի, մշտատեւորէն բարերար հետեւանքներով։ Ան Հնարեց մեր այբուբենը, մեր գիրերը, 406 Թուականին։ Իր չնորհիւ Հայ լեզուն ունեցաւ տեւականացման ամուր Հիմ եւ ինքնուրոյն գրականութիւն։

Սուրբ Մեսրոպ ծնած էր Տարօնի Հացեկաց դիւղին մէջ 353-ին ու վախճանած՝ 440ին։ Իր մարմինը Թաղուած է Օշականի մէջ, եւ իր դամբարանը Հայոց համար եղած է անվերջ ներշնչումի սրբավայր մը։

Իբրեւ դարգացած եւ լեզուագէտ աշխարհական, ան նախ պաշտօնավարեց արքունիքին մէջ, բայց յետոյ նուիրուեցաւ եկեղեցիին ու վարդապետ ձեռնադրուեցաւ։ Ան ցաւով տեսաւ թէ եկեղեցիներու մէջ Աստուածաչունչը Հայերէն չէր կարդացուեր, այլ յունարէն կամ ասորերէն ու կը Թարգմանուէր Հայերէնի։ Չդաց Հայ դիրեր ունենալու անՀրաժեշտութիւնը, եւ Սուրբ Սահակ իմաստուն կաթողիկոսին եւ Վռամշապուհ բարի Թագաւորին քաջալերութեամբ, ան Հնարեց մեր լեզուին յատուկ դիրերը։

Սուրբ Մեսրոպ ու Սահակ Հայրապետ, բազմաթիւ աշակերտներով, անմիջապէս ձեռնարկեցին Սուրբ Գիրքին Թարգմանութեան, որ իր վերջնական ձեւին մէջ, կոչուեցաւ «Թագուհին Թարգմանութեանց», իր լեզուին դեղեցկութեան եւ Թարգմանութեան Հարազատութեան համար։

Այդ ուսեալ, կրծնաւոր Հայրերուն աննման Հոյլը ստեղծեց մեր դասական գրականութեան Ոսկեդարը։

Սուրբ Մեսրոպ՝ ո՛չ միայն Հայ դիրի մշակներուն, այլ նաեւ բովանդակ ազդին պաշտելի սուրբն է, բոլոր դարերու Հայոց կեանքին խառնուած անմաՀօրէն։

ՄՈՎՍԵՍ ԽՈՐԵՆԱՑԻ

Եգական դէմք մըն է նաեւ Մովսես Խորենացի, որուն Հան
դէպ երախտիքի անսահման պարտք մը ունին իր ազգակիցները։
Նպատաը դող ան բերած է մեր գրականութեան անդին է։ Ան մեր
առաջին պատմագիրն է։ Այդ պատճառով ան կոչուած է «պատ
մահայը», մեր պատմաբաններուն հայրը։ Ան ջանացած է գրել
Հայոց պատմութիւնը, մեր ցեղին ծագումէն մինչեւ հրդ դար,
իր օրերը։

Խորենացին Սուրբ Մեսրոպի կրտսեր աշակերտներէն էր։
Ան դիտէր յունարէն եւ ասորերէն, իր ուսումը առած ըլլալով
Աղեքսանդրիոյ, Պոլսոյ եւ Եդեսիոյ մէջ, ու Հռոմ էր իր ժա
մանակին գիտութեանց։ Ան լաւ պատրաստուած գիտնական մըն
էր երբ ձեռնարկեց իր «Հայոց Պատմութիւնը» գրելու։ Արդիա
կան պատմագիրի մը պէս ան դիմեց բոլոր կարելի աղբիւրներուն
տեղեկութիւն Հաւաքելու։ Իր դիրքը լեցուն է սակայն անվաւեր
եղելութիւններով, աւապելներով, ժողովրդական բանատեղ
ծութեան թանկագին պատառիկներով, որոնք առանց իր այս
երկին կորսուած պիտի ըլլային առ յաւէտ։ Պատմութիւն եւ բա
նաստեղծութիւն մեծ Հրապոյրով իրարու կը խառնուին իր մեղի
ընծայած այս դանձարանին մէջ։

Այս պատճառով ան կոչուած է նաեւ «Թերթողահայը», մեր
բանաստեղծներուն Հայրը։

Իր «Հայոց Պատմութիւնը» ազդային Հպարտութիւն եւ գի
տակցութիւն արթնցուց իր օրերու Հայերուն Հոգիներուն մէջ։
Ան չարունակած է Հայրենասիրական նոյն զգացումները ար
թընցնել բոլոր դարերու Հայոց մէջ, որոնք անոր մէջ կը գանեն
իրենց նախահայրերուն քաջագործութեան ու առաքինութեան
գործերը։

139

CONVERSATIONAL: ԽՕՍԱԿՑԱԿԱՆ

ԾԱՆՕԹԱՆԱՆՔ — LET US GET ACQUAINTED

Ի՞նչ է ձեր անունը	What is your name?
Անունս Գրիգոր է	My name is Krikor.
Ի՞նչ է ձեր մականունը	What is your family name?
Մականունս Մասիսեան է	My family name is Massissian.
Ո՞ւր կը բնակիք	Where do you live?
Նիւ Եորք կը բնակիմ	I live in New York.
Ե՞րբ եկաք Նիւ Եորք	When did you c o m e to New York?
Տասը տարի առաջ	Ten years ago.
Ամերիկեան քաղաքացի՞ էք	Are you an American citizen?
Այո՛, հինգ տարիէ ի վեր	Yes, for five years.
Ամուսնացա՞ծ էք	Are you married?
Ո՛չ, ամուսնացած չեմ, ամուրի եմ։ Իսկ դո՞ւք	No, I am not married, I am a bachelor. And you?
Այո՛, ամուսնացած եմ	Yes, I am married.
Զաւակներ ունի՞ք	Have you any children?
Այո՛, երկու զաւակ ունիմ, մանչ մը եւ աղջիկ մը, դպրոց կ՚երթան	Yes, I have two children: a boy and a girl, they go to school.
Տունի՞ մը մէջ կը բնակիք	Do you live in a house?
Ո՛չ, յարկաբաժինի մը մէջ	No, in an apartment.
Քանի՞ սենեակ ունիք	How many rooms have you?

140

Հինգ սենեակ ունինք, հիւրանոց մը երկու ննջասենեակ, խոհանոց մը, եւ լոգարան մը	We have five rooms: a parlor, two bedrooms, one kitchen, and a bathroom.
Շատ բարեկամներ ունի՞ք	Have you many friends?
Այո, շատ բարեկամներ ունինք, որոնք կ՚այցելեն մեզի	Yes, we have many friends who visit us.
Յաճախ թատրոն կ՚երթա՞ք	Do you often go to the theater?
Երբեմն, նաեւ շարժանկարներու	Sometimes, also to the movies.
Երաժշտութիւն կը սիրէ՞ք	Do you like music?
Շատախագին. յաճախ նուագահանդէսներու կ՚երթանք	Very much. We often go to concerts.
Ի՞նչ տեսակ նուագ կը սիրէք	What kind of music do you like?
Դասական երաժշտութիւն	Classical music.
Ձեր զաւակներն ալ ձեզի հե՞տ կուգան	Do your children also come with you?
Ոչ, շատ պզտիկ են	No, they are too small.
Կը սիրէ՞ք կարդալ	Do you like to read?
Խիստ շատ, միշտ կը կարդանք	Exceedingly, we read all the time!
Շատ գիրք ունի՞ք տունը	Have you many books at home?
Երկու հազարէ աւելի, բայց մատենադարանէն ալ երբեմն փոխ կ՚առնենք	More than two thousand but we also borrow from the library.
Ի՞նչ կը կարդաք	What do you read?
Նախ առաւօտեան եւ երեկոյեան թերթ մը, եւ յետոյ գիրքեր	First a morning and an evening paper, and then books.
Ի՞նչ տեսակ գիրքեր	What kind of books?
Վէպեր, բանաստեղծութիւն, թատերախաղեր եւ գիտական գիրքեր	Novels, poetry, plays, and scientific books.
Առաւօտուն ժամը քանի՞ին կ՚ելլէք	At what time do you get up in the morning?
Ընդհանրապէս եօթին	Generally at seven o'clock.
Ժամը քանի՞ին կը նախաճաշէք	At what time do you breakfast?

141

Ժամը ութին

At eight o'clock.

Ի՞նչ կ՚ուտէք

What do you eat?

Պտուղի հիւթ, հաւկիթ, խաշ-
կած հաց, կարագ եւ սուրճ

Fruit juice, eggs, toasted bread,
butter and coffee.

Ի՞նչ է ձեր զբաղումը, բժի՞շկ
էք, փաստաբա՞ն, գրագէ՞տ,
լրագրո՞ղ

What is your occupation? Are
you a physician, a lawyer, a
writer, a journalist?

Վաճառական մըն եմ

I am a merchant.

Ժամը քանի՞ին գործի կ՚երթաք

At what time do you go to work?

իննին եւ վեցին կը վերադառնամ

At nine and return at six.

Ժամը քանի՞ին կը ճաշէք

At what time do you dine?

Ժամը եօթին

At seven o'clock.

Ճաշէ առաջ րմպելի մը կ՚առ-
նէ՞ք

Do you take a drink before
dinner?

Ոչ սովորաբար

Not habitually.

Կը ծխէ՞ք

Do you smoke?

Երբեք, վնասակար եւ ծախսալից
սովորութիւն մըն է

Never! That is a harmful and
costly habit.

Ճաշէն յետոյ ի՞նչ կ՚ընէք

What do you do after dinner?

Ընդհանրապէս տունը կը մնանք,
կը խօսակցինք, կը կարդանք,
պատկերասփիւռ կը դիտենք
կամ լաւ ձայնապնակներ կ՚ունկ-
նդրենք

Generally we stay at home, we
converse, we read, we watch
television or l i s t e n to good
records.

Այցելութեան կ՚երթա՞ք

Do you go visiting?

Այո, եւ յաճախ բարեկամներ կը
հրաւիրենք

Yes, and we often invite friends.

ՀԱՆԴԻՊՈՒՄ, ԱՅՑԵԼՈՒԹԻՒՆ — MEETING, VISITING

Բարի լոյս, Պարոն, Տիկին...
ի՞նչպէս էք

Good morning, Sir, Madam, how
are you?

Շատ լաւ, շնորհակալ եմ

I am very well, thank you.

Ի՞նչպէ՞ս է օդը այսօր

How is the weather today?

142

Ցուրտ է, պիտի ձիւնէ։ Երէկ ան-
ձրեւեց, խոնաւ եւ անհաճոյ
էր

It is cold, it will snow. Yesterday it rained, it was damp and disagreeable.

Օդը ի՞նչպէս է այս քաղաքին
մէջ ընդհանրապէս

How is the weather in this city generally?

Ընդհանրապէս մեղմ եւ հա-
ճելի է

Generally it is mild and agreeable.

Այսօր ցուրտ է. պիտի ուզէի՞ք
կրակին մօտ նստիլ

Today it is cold, would you like to sit near the fire?

Ոչ, բայց ուրախութեամբ գա-
ւաթ մը թէյ պիտի առնէի

No, but I would gladly take a cup of tea.

Կաթո՞վ թէ լեմոնով

With milk or lemon?

Քիչ մը կաթ եւ լեմոն

A little milk and lemon.

Ինչպէ՞ս է ձեր տիկինը

How is your wife?

Շնորհակալ եմ, լաւ է

Thank you she is well.

Այսօր ի՞նչ ըրիք

What did you do today?

Կարգ մը բաներ գնեցի. Ծնունդը
մօտ է

I bought certain things; Christmas is near.

Ի՞նչ գնեցի՞ք

What did you buy?

Տղաքներուն համար նուէրներ,
պատկերազարդ գիրքեր, խա-
ղալիքներ, պուպրիկներ եւ
երեկտրական կառախումբ մը։
Դուք ալ նուէրներ գնեցի՞ք։

I bought presents for the children. Illustrated books, toys, dolls, and an electric train. Did you also buy presents?

Այո, այսօր ամուսինիս համար
վզնոց մը, հովանոց մը, ձորդ
մը ձեռնոց եւ երկու գիրք
գնեցի։

Yes, today I bought for my husband a scarf, an umbrella, a pair of gloves and two books.

Ի՞նչպէս եկաք, ձեր կառ-
քո՞վ

How did you come? With your car?

Ոչ, մեր կառքը գիւղը թողու-
ցինք, հանրակառքով եկայ։

No, we left our car in the country, I came by bus.

Արդարեւ դժուար է կառք պա-
հել քաղաքը. տեղ չկայ գնե-
լու։

It is, indeed, difficult to keep a car in the city, there is no parking space.

Պէտք է որ շուտով մեկնիմ, ժամը քանի՞ է․	I must leave soon, what time is it?
Հինգ ու կէսն է	It is half past five.
Ժամացոյցնիդ առա՞ջ կ՚երթայ	Is your watch fast?
Ոչ, ո՛չ առաջ, ո՛չ ետ կ՚երթայ, ճիշդ է	No, it is neither fast nor slow: it is exact.
Այս ամառ պիտի ճամբորդէ՞ք	Will you travel this summer?
Այո, Եւրոպա երթալ մտադիր ենք	Yes, we intend to go to Europe.
Ո՞ր երկիրները պիտի այցելէք	Which countries will you visit?
Նախ Ֆրանսա, ուր ամիս մ՚ը պիտի մնամ, յետոյ մինչեւ Հայաստան, ուր կ՚ուզեմ հայերէն հասկնալ ու խօսիլ կարենալ։	First, France where I shall stay a month, then as far as Armenia, w h e r e I wish to be able to understand and speak Armenian.
Շոգենաւո՞վ պիտի երթաք թէ օդանաւով	Will you go by boat or by airplane?
Շոգենաւը հաճելի է բայց օդանաւով պիտի ճամբորդեմ․ աւելի արագ է եւ ծովախտի ենթակայ եմ։	The boat is agreeable but I shall travel by airplane. It is more rapid and I get sea-sick.
Գործի՞ ճամբորդութիւն մ՚ըն է թէ՝ հաճոյքի	Is it a business or pleasure trip?
Երկուքն ալ	Both.
Ձեր անցագիրը առա՞ծ էք	Have you obtained your passport?
Այո, եւ արդէն տեղս ալ ապահոված եմ օդանաւին վրայ	Yes, and I have already reserved my place on the plane.
Պանդո՞կ մ՚ը պիտի մնաք թէ ոչ՝ ազգականներու քով	Will you live in a hotel or with relatives?
Պանդոկը կը նախընտրեմ, մարդ աւելի ազատ կը զգայ	I prefer the hotel, one feels freer.
Բարեկամներ ունի՞ք այնտեղ	Have you any friends there?
Ոչ, մարդ չեմ ճանչնար	No, I know no one.

144

Այս առաջի՞ն անգամն է որ Եւ֊
րոպա կ՛երթաք

Is this the first time that you are going to Europe?

Ո՛չ, երկրորդ անգամն է

No, it is the second time.

Բարի ճամբորդութի՛ւն։ Երբ որ ժամանակ ունենաք բացիկ մը ղրկեցէք ինծի։

Bon voyage! Whenever you have time send me a postcard.

Ուրախութեամբ

Gladly.

Ե՞րբ մեզ տեսնել պիտի գաք դարձեալ։ Ձեր այցելութիւնը շատ կարճ եղաւ։

When will you come to see us again? Your visit was too short.

Հիմա կարգը ձերն է մեզ տեսնել գալու. Հաճոյքով կը սպա֊ սենք. մնա՛ք բարով։

It is now your turn to come to see us; we look forward to it with pleasure. Goodbye!

Երթաք բարով։ Յարգանքներս ձեր տիկինին։

Goodbye! My regards to your wife.

ԱՄԱՌ, ԳԻՒՂ   SUMMER, COUNTRY

Ամառը ո՞ւր կ՛անցընէք. ծովե֊ զե՞րբը թէ ո՛չ լերը.

Where do you spend the summer, at the seashore or in the mountain?

Սովրաբար լեռը

Ordinarily in the mountain.

Պանդո՞կ մը կ՛երթաք

Do you go to a hotel?

Ո՛չ, հիւղակ մը ունինք, դաշտե֊ րուն մէջ, լեռան մը ստորոտը։

No, we have a cottage, in the fields, at the foot of a mountain.

Պարտէզ մը ունի՞ք

Have you a garden?

Այո, կինս շատ կը սիրէ ծա֊ ղիկներ մշակել

Yes, my wife likes to cultivate flowers very much.

Ի՞նչ տեսակ ծաղիկներ ունիք

What kind of flowers have you?

Ունինք վարդեր, լեղակներ, մար֊ գարտածաղիկներ եւ գարնան՝ մանիշակներ։

We have roses, lilacs, daisies, and in the spring violets.

Թանջարանոց մ՚ըն ալ ունի՞ք

Այո, պզտիկ մ՚ը․ լոլիկ, վարունգ, հազար, թարմ լուբիա եւ ստեպղին կը հասցնենք։

Շատ արեւ ունի՞ք

Մինչեւ ժամը տասնեկմէ կ․ շատ ծառեր ունինք տունին շուրջը։

Ձեր տնակը զով ըլլալու է տաք օրերուն։

Այո, շատ հաճելի է որովհետեւ ծառերը զով կը պահեն տունը

Ո՞րն է ամէնէն տաք ամիսը

Յուլիս ամիսը, կարծեմ

Ե՞րբ դիրղ կ՚երթաք

Յունիսի սկիզբը

Մինչեւ ե՞րբ հոն կը մնաք

Մինչեւ Սեպտեմբերի վերջը ընդհանրապէս

Ամառը չէ՞ք աշխատիր

Այո, կ՚աշխատիմ, բայց քաղաքը կը մնամ։ Շաբաթավերջերուն դիրղ կ՚երթամ։

Արձակուրդ չէ՞ք առներ

Այո, տասնեւհինգ օր միայն

Գիւղը գեղեցիկ է, չէ՞

Հրաշալի, մանաւանդ աշունը որ ամէնէն աղուոր եղանակն է ըստ իս։

Ես գարունը կը նախընտրեմ երբ ամէն ինչ վերստին կը ծնի։ Ձմեռն ալ կը սիրեմ իր մարզախաղերուն համար

Have you also a vegetable garden?

Yes, a small one; we grow tomatoes, cucumbers, lettuce, spring beans and carrots.

Have you much sunlight?

Until eleven o'clock, we have many trees around the cottage.

Your cottage must be cool during the hot days.

Yes, it is very agreeable because the trees keep the house cool.

Which is the hottest month?

The month of July, I think.

When do you go to the country?

At the beginning of June.

Until when do you stay there?

Until the end of September generally.

Don't you work during the summer?

Yes, I do, but I stay in the city. I go to the country for the week-ends.

Don't you take a vacation?

Yes, only fifteen days.

The country is beautiful, isn't it?

Splendid, especially in autumn which is the most beautiful season in my opinion.

I prefer the spring when all is born again. I also like the winter for its sports.

146

Եկէ՛ք մեզ տեսնել դիւղը յաշորդ
ամառ. կրնանք կոլֆ խաղալ
եւ մեր կիներն ալ թէնիս. Մենք
ունինք նաեւ լճակ մը ուր պզ-
տիկները կրնան լողալ

Ուրիշ ի՞նչ հրապուրիչ բաներ
ունիք

Սքանչելի նուագահանդէսներ
ունինք, ամառնային թատրոն
մը եւ շատ մը հնօրեայ առար-
կաներու խանութներ

Ձեր տեղը շատ հրապուրիչ կը
թուի

Մենք ծովեզերք կ՚երթանք ու
մեր միակ մարզախաղը նա-
ւարկութիւն է

Come and see us in the country
next summer. We can play
golf and our wives tennis. We
also have a small lake where
the children can swim.

What other attractions have
you?

We have excellent concerts, a
summer theater and many an-
tique shops.

Your place seems very attrac-
tive.

We go to the beach and our only
sport is boating.

ԹԱՏՐՈՆԸ · THE THEATER

Երկու տոմս, եթէ կը հաճիք

Ո՞ր կարգը

Որքան որ կարելի է բեմին մօտ.
կ՚ուզենք լաւ տեսնել ու լսել

Երկու տեղ ունինք երրորդ կարգը

Լաւ, ի՞նչ է գինը

Տասը տոլար երկուքին համար

Ո՞ր ժամուն վարագոյրը կը բաց-
ուի

Իննին քառորդ մնացած կամ
իննին

Ուրեմն շատ ատեն ունինք ճաշելու. դուրս ելլենք

Two tickets, please.

Which row?

As near the stage as possible. We
want to see well and hear well.

We have two seats in the third
row.

Fine, what is the price?

Ten dollars for the two.

At what time does the curtain
go up?

At quarter to nine or nine
o'clock.

We therefore have plenty of time
to eat. Let us go out.

147

Ո՞ր ճաշարանը երթանք

To which restaurant shall we go?

Ամէնէն մօտիկը, որպէսզի կա— րենանք քալել

The nearest one so that we may walk.

Այո, չ՚արժեր կառքը դուրս հա— նել կառատունէն

Yes, it is not worth while to take the car out of the garage.

Չինական ճաշարան մը կայ փո— ղոցին անկիւնը, հոն երթանք

There is a Chinese restaurant at the corner of this street, let us go there.

Չինական կերակուր կը սիրէ՞ք

Do you like Chinese food?

Այո, դիւրաւ կը մարսուին եւ չեն գիրցներ

Yes, it is easily digested and is not fattening.

Հոն երթանք, քանի որ ձեզի հա— ճելի է

Let us go there, since it pleases you.

Ահաւասիկ ճաշարանը

Here is the restaurant.

Երկու վայրկեանէն հոս եկանք

It took us two minutes to come here.

Մեր Վահան բարեկամը հոս է. ի՞նչ կ՚ընէք այստեղ

Here is our friend Vahan. What are you doing here?

Եկած եմ ճաշելու, ձեզի պէս

I have come to eat, like you.

Գո՞ւք այլ արդեօք եկած էք տես— նելու այն խաղը զոր մենք պի— տի տեսնենք

Have you by any chance come also to see the play which we shall see?

Ի՞նչ խաղ պիտի տեսնէք. Սա— րոյեա՞նին խաղը

What play will you see? The play by Saroyan?

Այո, ի՞նչ զուգադիպութիւն

Yes, what a coincidence!

Կ՚ըսեն թէ շատ գեղեցիկ է

They say that it is very beautiful.

Սարոյեանին բոլոր թատերախա— ղերն ալ լաւ են։ Անոր կարճ պատմուածքներն ալ կը սիրեմ

All the plays of Saroyan are fine. I like his short stories also.

Բոլորն ալ կարդացած չեմ բայց քոյրս մեծ ընթերցող մըն է ու զանոնք շատ կը սիրէ

I have not read them all but my sister is a great reader and she likes them very much.

Իր թատերախաղերէն ոչ մէկը դեռ տեսած ենք։ Ասիկա առաջինը պիտի ըլլայ

We have not yet seen any of his plays. This will be the first one.

Գիտէ՞ք թէ որոնք են դերասանները

Do you know who the actors are?

Ոչ, չմտածեցինք յայտագիր մը առնել

No, we did not think of getting a program.

Քաղա՞քը պիտի մնաք այս գիշեր

Will you stay in the city for the night.

Ոչ, այս գիշեր իսկ պիտի վերադառնամ Գոնէթիքըթ, իսկ դո՞ւք

No, I shall return this very night to Connecticut, and you?

Ես պանդոկ մը պիտի մնամ։ Կինս վաղը պիտի գայ ինծի միանալու քանի մը բաներ գնելու համար

I shall stay in a hotel. My wife is coming tomorrow to join me to buy a few things.

ԲԺԻՇԿԸ   THE DOCTOR

Բարի լոյս, Պրն. Գասպարեան

Good morning, Mr. Kasbarian!

Բարի լոյս, Պրն. Արաւեան

Good morning, Mr. Aravian!

Ի՞նչ ունիք, յոգնած կ՚երեւաք

What is the matter with you? You look tired.

Չեմ գիտեր ճշդիւ թէ ինչ ունիմ

I don't know exactly what I have.

Տենդ ունի՞ք

Have you a fever?

Չեմ կարծեր

I don't think so.

Ինչո՞ւ բժիշկին չէք երթար

Why don't you go to the doctor?

Կ՚ատեմ դեղերը

I hate medicines.

Ես ալ շատ աղէկ չեմ զգար

I also don't feel quite well.

Եկո՛ւր, միասին բժիշկին երթանք

Come, let us go to the d o c t o r together.

Գէշ գաղափար մը չէ

It is not a bad idea.

149

Նախ թժիշկին կ'երթանք, եւ
յետոյ, եթէ մեզ անկողին
շդրկէ, կրնանք ճաշարան մը
ճաշել ու թերեւս թատերախաղ
մը երթալ տեսնել եթէ կրնանք
տոմսակ գտնել:
Հիանալի գաղափար․ այսպէս
ճաճոյքը ցաւին պիտի խառ-
նենք եւ դժ յիշատակ մը պի-
տի չպահենք այսօրէն
Բարեւ, Տոքթ․ Յուսիկեան
Բարեւ, Պրն․ Կարապետեան,
խնդրեմ, նստեցէ՛ք եւ ըսէ՛ք
թէ ի՛նչ կը զգաք
Հարբուխ մը ունիմ ու ցաւեր բոլոր մարմինիս վրայ
Տեսնենք թէ ջերմաչափը ի՛նչ
կ'ըսէ: ... Տենդ չունիք, ախոր-
ժակնի°դ ինչպէս է
Ալեղծ
Լաւ կը քնանա°ք
Այս վերջին քանի մը օրերը լաւ
չկրցայ քնանալ
Հանուեցէ՛ք․ կ'ուզեմ քննել ձեզ:
Լուրջ բան մը չունիք: Ասա-
ւասիկ դեղագիրս: Այս դեղա-
հատերը առէք, երեք ժամը
անգամ մը հատ մը, եւ երկու
կամ երեք օրէն ինքգինքինիդ
պիտի գտնէք
Շնորհակալ եմ, տոքթըր: Բարե-
կամս, Պրն․ Առաւեանը, դուր-
սը կը սպասէ․ ան ալ կ'ուզէ
քննուիլ ձեզմէ: Կը յուսամ
նոյնքան քաջալերական լուրեր
պիտի տաք անոր որքան տուիք
ինծի: Մնաք բարեւ, կրկին
շնորհակալութիւն

150

ԳՐԱՏՈՒՆԸ   THE BOOKSTORE

Արձակուրդով կը մեկնիմ։ Կ'ու
զեմ քանի մը գիրք տանիլ
հետս

I am leaving on vacation. I want to take a few books with me.

Ի՞նչ տեսակ գիրքեր

What kind of books?

Վէպեր, կենսագրութիւններ եւ
արկածախնդրութեան պատ
մութիւն մը

Novels, biographies, and an adventure story.

Լո՞ւրջ թէ ոչ թեթեւ վէպեր կը
սիրէք

Do you like serious or light novels?

Լուրջ վէպերը կը նախընտրեմ,
ընդհանրապէս, բայց եթէ թե
թեւ վէպերը սրամտութեամբ
գրուած են, չեմ արհամարհեր
զանոնք։ Օրուան օրուան մը աշ
խատութենէն յետոյ, հանգիստ
կը պատճառեն

I prefer the serious novels, as a rule, but if light novels are written wittily I do not disdain them. After a day's hard work they are relaxing.

Մէկ կամ երկու լաւ ինքնակեն
սագրութիւն ունինք ու նաեւ
ամենավերջին թատերախաղե
րը։ Երկու վէպեր ալ ունինք,
որոնք պիտի հետաքրքրեն ձեզ
եթէ քաղաքականութեամբ կը
հետաքրքրուիք

We have one or two good autobiographies and also the latest plays. We also have two novels which will interest you if you are interested in politics.

Քաղաքականութեամբ կը չահա
գրգռուիմ բայց կ'ուզեմ մոռ
նալ զայն արձակուրդիս ատեն։
Ոստիկանական պատմութիւն
ներ ալ ունի՞ք

I am interested in politics but I prefer to forget it during my vacations. Have you also detective stories?

Այո, այս գիրքերը կ'ուզէ՞ք որ
մենք ձեզի ղրկենք։ Բաւական
մեծ ծրար մը պիտի ըլլայ։
Ձեր կառքը հետերնի՞դ է

Yes. Do you wish us to send these books to you? It will be quite a big package. Is your car with you?

Ոչ, անկարելի է կառքով շրջա-
գայիլ հինգէն յետոյ։ Կ՚աղա-
չեմ ծրարը տունս ուղեցէք։
Հասցէս ունիք։

Հաճոյքով․ Ե՞րբ պիտի մեկնիք

Դէպի ամիսին կէսին

Անպահ ովարար առէ տառշ պիտի
ստանաք դայն

No. It is impossible to travel in
a car after five. Please send
the package to my house. You
have my address.

With pleasure. When will you
leave?

Towards the middle of the
month.

You will surely receive it before
then.

ՈՒՍԱՆՈՂՆԵՐ   STUDENTS

Բարեւ, Արաքսի

Բարեւ Հայկազ, ի՞նչպէս ես

Շնորհակալ եմ, շատ աղէկ, բայց
անշուշտ շատ զբաղ աւարտա-
կան քննութիւններու պատ-
ճառաւ

Երկուքս ալ նոյն դժուարու-
թեանց մէջէն կ՚անցնինք․
վայրկեան մը հանգիստ չու-
նիմ։ Երէկ ուսողութիւնն էր,
այսօր պատմութիւն

Մենք երէկ ունեցանք մեր պատ-
մութեան քննութիւնը։ Այսօր
գիտութիւններ։ Ո՞ր գոլէճր կը
կարծէք թէ պիտի երթաք

Դիմումներ իրր զանազան գոլէճ-
երու եւ կը սպասեմ իրենց պա-
տասխանին ընդրութիւնս ընե-
լու համար

Իմ ընդրութիւնս Եէյլր պիտի
ըլլար, եթէ այդ կարելի լինէր

Hi, Araxi!

Hi, Haygaz! How are you?

Thanks, quite well but of course
very b u s y on account of the
final examinations.

Both of us are passing through
the same difficulties. I have
not a minute of leisure. Yesterday it was math, today
history.

We had our history exam yesterday, today sciences. To what
college do you think you will
go?

I sent applications to several
colleges and I am waiting for
their answers to make my
choice.

My choice would be Yale, if that
were possible.

152

Ի՞նչ պիտի ըլլայ ձեր գլխաւոր In what will you major?
ճիւղը

Քաղաքական գիտութիւններ. կը Political sciences. I would like
փափաքիմ դիւանագիտութեան to enter diplomacy.
մէջ մտնել

Լաւ ասպարէզ մըն է: Իմ եղ- It is a good career. My brother
բայրս կը պատրաստուի ճար- is preparing himself to be an
տարագէտ ըլլալու: Հիւլէա- engineer. We are in the atom-
կան դարուն մէջ ենք ic age.

Իսկ դո՞ւք, որոշա՞ծ էք թէ ի՛նչ And you? Have you decided
պիտի ըլլայ ձեր մասնագի- what your specialty will be?
տութը

Օտար լեզուներ, ու ապագանելու Foreign languages, to teach if
համար, եթէ պէտք ըլլայ: necessary. But to tell you
Բայց ճշմարիտը ըսելու հա- the truth I prefer the home
մար, կը նախընտրեմ տո'ւնը as a career. I would like to
իբրեւ ասպարէզ: Կ'ուզեմ ըն- form a family, raise children.
տանիք մը կազմել, զաւակներ It is not original! But per-
մեծցընել: Ինքնատիպ չէ, haps it is more difficult and
բայց թերեւս աւելի դժուար է essential.
եւ էական

ԼՐԱԳԻՐՆԵՐ   NEWSPAPERS

Ո՞ր յօդուածները կը հետաքրքր- Which articles interest you
բեն ձեզ ամէնէն աւելի most?

Նախ, օրուան լուրերը, յետոյ First, the news of the day, then
խմբագրականները, եւ յետոյ the editorials and then the
կարգ մը սիւնակագիրներու views of certain columnists.
տեսութիւնները

Ամենավերջին գիրքերու մասին Do you read reviews on the latest
գրախօսականներ կը կարդա՞ք books?

Այո, եւ կը կարդամ նաեւ թա- Yes, and I also read the theatri-
տերական քրոնիկներ cal reviews.

153

Արտաքին քաղաքականութեամբ
կը հետաքրքրուի՞ք
Չափազանց, քանի որ ո'չ մէկ
ազգ կրնայ կղզիացած կեանք
մը ապրիլ այսօր

Are you interested in foreign politics?

Very much so, since no nation can live an isolated life to'day.

Իսկ ներքի՞ն քաղաքականու-
թեամբ

And how about internal politics?

Ծիշտ նոյնքան, բնականաբար։
Կը հետեւիմ դէպքերու ըն-
թացքին, մեր քաղաքական
թեկնածուներու յայտարարու-
թիւնները կը կարդամ, իմաս-
տութեամբ կարենալ քուէար-
կելու համար։

Just as much, naturally. I follow the course of events, read the statements of our political candidates in order to be able to vote wisely.

Թերթերը կարդալ արդարեւ էական է եւ մամուլին դերը կեն-
սական։

To read the newspapers is, indeed, essential and the role of the press vital.

ԿԻՐԱԿԻ ԱՌԱՒOS   SUNDAY MORNING

Բարի լոյս, մա՛յր
Բարի լոյս, որդեա'ս
Ուշ արթնցայ, պէտք է աճա-
պարեմ

Good morning, mother.
Good morning, my son.
I woke up late, I must hurry.

Նախաճաշդ պատրաստ է

Your breakfast is ready.

Կրնաս անմիջապէս ուտել ու ե-
կեղեցի երթալ, պատարագին
հասնիլ

You can eat immediately, go to church and be in time for the Mass.

Այո', պէտք է որ 10ին հոն ըլլամ,
քանի որ երգիչ խումբին մէջն
եմ

Yes, I must be there at ten since I am in the choir.

Դուն ալ պիտո դա°ս ինձի հետ

Are you coming with me?

Այո', քոյրդ ալ. հայրդ արդէն
գնաց, մ'իշտ կ'աճապարէ գի-
տես։

Yes, your sister also; your father has already gone; he is always in a hurry as you know!

Բոյրդ պէտք է Կիրակնօրեայ
վարժարանը թողունք: Ո՞վ
պիտի պատարագէ այսօր:

We must leave your sister at the
Sunday School. Who is to of-
ficiate at Mass today?

Առաջնորդ Հայրը․ Զատիկ է այսօր, պիտի քարոզէ ալ:

The Archbishop prelate, it is
Easter today, he will also de-
liver the sermon.

Ուրեմն շատ բազմութիւն պիտի
ըլլայ:

There will be a big crowd
then?

Անշուշտ: Եկեղեցիէն յետոյ ի՞նչ
պիտի ընենք:

Of course. What are we going to
do after the church service.

Տուն պիտի վերադառնանք, Հոր-
եղբայրդ եւ Հորաքրոյրդ պիտի
գան, իրենց զաւակներով,
կարմիր Հաւկիթ պիտի կոտ-
րենք․․․

We shall return home, your un-
cle and aunt will come with
their children, we shall break
red eggs!

Իսկ ճաշէ՞ն վերջ

And what about after lunch?

Կրնաս զարմիկներուդ Հետ դուրս
ելլել:

You can go out with your cou-
sins.

Օդը լաւ է, կրնանք պտոյտ մը
ընել: Ես պատրաստ եմ հիմա,
երթա՛նք ։

The weather is fine, we can take
a walk. I am now ready, let
us go.

ԵՐԿՈՒ ՏԻԿԻՆՆԵՐ ԿԸ ԽՕՍԱԿՑԻՆ
TWO LADIES ARE CONVERSING

Նուագահանդէս պիտի երթա՞ք
յառաջիկայ Կիրակի

Are you going to the concert
next Sunday?

Ո՞ր նուագահանդէսին

Which concert?

Այն զոր տիկիններր կազմակեր-
պած են Առաջնորդարանին
համար

The one which the ladies have
organized for the Prelacy.

Այո, անցեալ տարի փայլուն
Հանդէս մըն էր

Yes, last year it was a brilliant
affair.

155

Ա՞ն ալ նուագահանդէս մըն էր

Ոչ, թատերախաղ մըն էր. Հե-
տաքրքրաշարժ էր եւ դուրա-
ճալի էր դերասաններն ու դե-
րասանուհիները տեսնել

Ինչո՞ւ. կը ճանչնայի՞ք զանոնք

Այո, բոլորն ալ մեր բարեկամ-
ներն էին, կազմակերպիչ
յանձնախումբին անդամներ

Թանձնախումբին անդա՞մ էք

Ոչ, մօրաքրոյրս է: Բոլոր տիկին-
ները անձնուիրօրէն կ'աշխա-
տին

Հիանալի են

Երկու շաբաթ վերջ Բարեգործա-
կանի տիկիններուն պարա-
հանդէսը կայ

Ան ալ միշտ փայլուն հանդէս մը
կ'ըլլայ: Թանձնախումբին ան-
դամները, նոյն տիկիննե՞րն
են

Ոչ, տարբեր խումբ մըն է, բայց
անոնք ալ նոյնքան եռանդով
ու նուիրումով կ'աշխատին

Կ'ենթադրեմ թէ հոն ալ զիրար
պիտի տեսնենք

Ապահովապար: Յտեսութիւն

Յտեսութիւն

Was it also a concert?

No, it was a play. It was in-
teresting and amusing to see
the actors and the actresses.

Why? Did you know them?

Yes, they were all our friends,
members of the organizing
committee.

Are you a member of the committee?

No, my aunt is. All the ladies
work devotedly.

They are admirable.

In two weeks there will be the
Ball of the AGBU Ladies.

That also is always a brilliant
affair. Are the members of
that committee the same ladies?

No, it is a different group, but
they also work just as dili-
gently and devotedly.

I suppose we shall see each other
there also.

Certainly. Goodbye until then.

Goodbye till then.

VOCABULARIES

ARMENIAN - ENGLISH

ազահ	greedy	ակամայ	unwillingly
ազարակ	farm	ականջ	ear
ագռաւ	crow	ակնարկ	glance
ադամանդ	diamond	ակնոց	eyeglasses
ազատ	free	ակնկալել	to expect
ազատական	liberal	ակումբ	club
ազատել	to free	ակռայ	tooth
ազատութիւն	liberty	ահա, ահաւասիկ	here is
ազատօրէն	freely	ահաբեկել	to terrorize
ազգ	nation	ահագին	enormous
ազգային	national	ահաւոր	terrible
ազդ	advertisement	ահեղ	terrific
ազդակ	factor	ահռելի	frightful
ազդարարել	to give notice	աղ	salt
ազդել	to influence	աղաղակ	cry
ազդեցիկ	influential	աղաղակել	to cry
ազդեցութիւն	influence	աղաչել	to beseech
ազդու	effective	աղբիւր	source, fountain
ազնիւ	kind	աղէկ	well
ազնուական	noble	աղէտ	disaster
ազնուօրէն	kindly	աղէտառ	disastrous
աթոռ	chair	աղի	salty
աժան	cheap	աղիւս	brick
ալիւր	flour	աղմկալի	noisy
ալիք	wave	աղմուկ	noise
ախոռ	stable	աղուոր	pretty
ախորժակ	appetite	աղջիկ	girl
ախորժելի	agreeable	աղտ	dirt
ախտ	disease	աղտոտ	dirty
ածական	adjective	աղտոտել	to dirty
ածելի	razor	աղօթել	to pray
ածիլել	to shave	աղօթք	prayer
ածիլուիլ	to be shaved	աղօտ	dim
ածուխ	coal	աղքատ	poor

159

աճապարանք	haste	*անասունակ*	unruly
աճապարել	to hasten	*անարատ*	pure
աճառ	soap	*անիրավ*	unjust
աճիլ	to grow	*անարիւն*	bloodless
աճումն	growth	*անարժան*	unworthy
ամայի	desert (adj.)	*անբաժան*	inseparable
աման	vessel, receptacle	*անբախտ*	unlucky
ամբարել	to amass	*անբան*	stupid
ամբողջ	whole, entire	*անբաւ*	boundless
ամբողջովին	entirely	*անբաւարար*	insufficient
ամէն	amen, every	*անբնական*	unnatural
ամիս	month	*անդադար*	time, even
ամուսին	husband	*անդին*	invaluable
ամուսնանալ	to get married	*անդթութիւն*	cruelty
ամուր	solid	*անդուղ*	cruel
ամուրի	bachelor	*անդամ*	member
ամչալ	to be ashamed	*անդունդ*	abyss
ամպ	cloud	*անդրադառնալ*	to revert
ամփոփ	concise	*անդրդուելի*	unshakable
ամօթ	shame	*անզոր*	powerless
այդ, այն	that (adj.)	*անէծք*	curse
այլազան	diverse	*անընդունելի*	unacceptable
այլապէս	otherwise	*անթափանց*	opaque
այնպէս	that way	*անթիւ*	innumerable
այնպէս որ	so that	*անիծել*	to curse
այնուհետեւ	after that	*անիմաստ*	meaningless
այնտեղ	there	*անիրական*	unreal
այո	yes	*անիրաւ*	unjust
այս	this	*անիւ*	wheel
այսքան	this much	*անլի*	saltless
այսօր	today	*անխելք*	stupid
այտ	cheek	*անխոնջ*	tireless
այր	male	*անխորտակելի*	indestructible
այրի	widow	*անկախ*	independent
այցելել	to visit	*անկախութիւն*	independence
այցելութիւն	visit	*անկայուն*	unstable
ան	he, she, it	*անկապ*	incoherent
անակնկալ	surprise	*անկարելի*	impossible
անապատ	desert	*անկարելիութիւն*	impossibility

160

անկարող	unable, incompetent
անկատար	imperfect
անկենդան	inanimate
անկիւն	angle
անկողին	bed
անկողմնակալ	impartial
անհանդուրժելի	intolerable
անհատ	individual
անհատականութիւն	individuality
անհարկի	unnecessary
անհոգ	careless
անհուն	immense
անհրաժեշտութիւն	necessity
անձ	person
անձամբ	in person, personally
անձնական	personal
անձնապէս	personally
անձնատուր ըլլալ	to surrender oneself
անձնաւորութիւն	personality
անձնուէր	devoted
անձրեւ	rain
անձրեւել	to rain
անմահ	immortal
անմահութիւն	immortality
անմիջապէս	immediately
անմիտ	stupid, sot
անմոռանալի	unforgettable
անյարմար	unsuitable
աններելի	unforgivable
աննիւթական	immaterial
աննշան	insignificant
անշարժ	immovable
անուանական	nominal
անուանի	reputable
անուշ	sweet
անչափ	immeasurable
անպատիւ	dishonorable
անպատկառ	impudent
անջատ	separate
անջնջելի	undestructible
անջրպետ, միջոց	space
անսովոր	unusual
անվախ	fearless
անտանելի	intolerable
անտառ	forest
անտարբեր	indifferent
անտարբերութիւն	indifference
անցաւոր	transitory
անցեալ	past
անցնիլ	to pass
անքուն	sleepless
աշխարհ	world
աշխարհաբար	modern Armenian language
աշխարհական	layman
աշխատիլ	to work
աշխատութիւն	work
աշուն	autumn
աշտարակ	tower
աչք	eye
ապագայ	future
ապակի	glass
ապահով	sure, secure
ապահովութիւն	security, assurance
ապաստան	refuge
ապացոյց	proof
ապացուցանել	to prove
ապուշ	stupid
ապրանք	merchandise
ապտակ	slap
ապտակել	to slap
ապրիլ	April
ապրիլ	to live

161

ապօրէն	illegitimate
առագաստ	sail
առագաստանաւ	sail boat
առած	proverb
առակ	fable
առանձին	alone
առանց	without
առանցք	axis
առաջ	before
առաջարկել	to propose
առաջին	first
առաջնորդ	leader, primate
առաջնորդել	to lead
առաջնորդարան	prelacy
առաջնորդութիւն	leadership
առասպել	legend
առաստաղ	ceiling
առարկայ	object
առարկայօրէն	objectively
առարկել	to object
առատ	abundant
առաւել	more, plus
առաւելութիւն	advantage
առաւօտ	morning
առաքեալ	apostle
առաքինի	virtuous
առեղծուած	enigma
առեւտուր	trade
առիթ	occasion
առիւծ	lion
առիւծասիրտ	lion hearted
առնել	to take
առողջ	healthy
առու, առուակ	stream, brook
աս, ասիկա	this
ասեղ	needle
ասպարէզ	career
ասպարէզ կարդալ	to challenge
աստիճան	degree

աստղ	star
աստեղագէտ,	astronomer
աստղագէտ	
աստղագուշ	astrologer
աստեղագիտու-	astronomy
թիւն	
աստղանաւորդ	astronaut
Աստուած	God
աստուածաբա-	theology
նութիւն	
աստուածային	divine
աստուածաշունչ	bible
ատաղձագործ	carpenter
ատել	to hate
ատելութիւն	hatred
ատեն	time
ատենապետ	chairman
ատենադպիր	secretary
արագ	quick, fast
արական	masculine
արատ	spot, stain
արարիչ	creator
արարք	act, deed
արբանեակ	satellite
արբենալ	to get drunk
արդար	just, righteous
արդէն	already
արդիւնք	result
արեգակ, արեւ	sun
արեւելեան	oriental, eastern
արեւելք	east
արեւմուտք	west
արեւմտեան	western
արթննալ	to wake up
արթնցնել	to awaken
արթուն	awake
արժանի	worthy
արժանիք	merit
արժէք	value

162

արի	brave
արիւն	blood
արիւնարբու	bloodthirsty
արկած	accident
արկածալի	adventurous
արկածախնդիր	adventurer
արկածախնդ-րութիւն	adventure
արհամարհել	despise
արհեստ	craft
արհեստաւոր	artisan, craftsman
արձակ	prose
արձակագիր	prose writer
արձակել	to liberate, set free
արձակուրդ	vacation
արձան	statue
արձանագործ	sculptor
արձանագործու-թիւն	sculpture
արձանագրու-թիւն	record
արմատ	root
արմատական	radical
արմատախիլ	uprooted
արմատապէս	radically
արշալոյս	dawn
արշաւ	campaign
արշաւանք	invasion
արշաւել	to invade
արու	male
արուարձան	suburb
արուեստ	art
արուեստագէտ	artist
արտադրել	to produce
արտածել	to export
արտածում	exportation
արտակարգ	extraordinary
արտասուել	to cry, to weep
արտաքին	external

արտորալ	to hasten
արտօնել	to authorize, **permit**
արցունք	tear
արքայ	king
արքայական	royal
արքայութիւն	kingdom, paradise
արքունիք	court (royal)
աւազ	sand
աւազան	basin, pool
աւաղ	alas
աւաղել	to regret
աւանդական	traditional
աւանդութիւն	tradition
աւարտել	to finish
աւել	broom
աւելի	more
աւելորդ	superfluous
աւելցնել	to increase
աւետարան	gospel
աւետարանիչ	evangelist
աւերակ	ruin
աւերել	to ruin
աւրել	to erase
աւիւն	ardor
ափ	palm, shore
ախ ու վախ	alas
ապտակ	kick
աքաղաղ, աքլոր	cock

Բ

բաբախել	to throb
բազմապատկել	to multiply
բազմութիւն	crowd
բազուկ	arm
բաժակ	cup
բաժակաճառ	speech for toast

163

բաժանում	division
բաժին	share
բաժանել	to divide
բախել	to knock
բախում	knock, conflict
բախտ	luck
բախտավոր	lucky, fortunate
բաղադրել	to compose
բաղաձայն	consonant
բաղդատել	to compare
բաղդատաբար	comparatively
բաղկանալ	to consist of
բաղձալ	to desire
բաղձալի	desirable
բաղձանք	desire
բաղնիք	bath
բամպակ	cotton
բայ	verb
բայց	but
բան	thing
բանալ	to open
բանալի	key
բանախոս	lecturer
բանախոսել	to lecture
բանախոսություն	lecture
բանակ	army
բանականություն	reason
բանակցել	to negotiate
բանաստեղծ	poet
բանաստեղծություն	poetry
բանավոր	reasonable
բանջարեղէն	vegetable
բանտ	prison
բանտարկյալ	prisoner
բանտարկել	to imprison
բառ	word
բառախաղ	pun
բառական	literal
բարակ	thin
բարեկամ	friend
բարդ	complicated
բարեբախտ	fortunate
բարեբախտաբար	fortunately
բարերարծ	benefactor
բարեգործական	benevolent
բարեգործություն	benevolence
բարելավել	to improve
բարեկարգել	to reform
բարեկիրթ	courteous
բարեհամբավ	of good repute
բարեպաշտ	pious
բարեսէր	charitable
բարերար	benefactor
բարեփոխել	to modify, improve
բարի	good
բարկանալ	to get angry
բարկություն	anger
բարձր	high
բարձրաձայն	loud
բարձրություն	height, altitude
բաց	open
բացակայ	absent
բացատրել	to explain
բացատրություն	explanation
բացառիկ	exceptional
բացառություն	exception
բացի	except
բավական	enough
բավել	to suffice
բեմ	platform
բերան	mouth
բերանացի	oral
բեռ	load
բերդ	fortress
բերել	to bring
բժիշկ	physician
բժշկական	medical

164

բժշկել	to cure
բիծ	spot, stain
բծախնդիր	meticulous
բնական	natural
բնակիչ	inhabitant
բնակչութիւն	population
բնութիւն	nature
բնաշրջում	evolution
բոլոր	all
բոլորակ	circle
բոյս	plant
բոյր	smell
բռնի	violent
բուսականութիւն	vegetation
բռնակալ	tyrant
բռնի	forcibly
բռնութիւն	violence
բրածոյ	fossil

Գ.

գագաթ	summit
գազան	wild beast
գալ	to come
գահ	throne
գաղափար	idea
գաղտնաբար	secretly
գաղտնիք	secret
գամ	nail
գայլ	wolf
գանգատ	complaint
գանգատիլ	to complain
գանձ	treasure
գանձապահ	treasurer
գարուն	spring
գաւազան	cane, stick

գաւաթ	cup
գաւառ	province
գաւառային	provincial
գգուանք	caress
գգուել	to caress
գեղարուեստ	fine art
գեղեցիկ	beautiful
գեղեցկութիւն	beauty
գետին	ground
գերազանց	superior
գերիշխան	sovereign
գերեզման	grave
գէթ	at least
գէշ	bad
գէր	fat
գիծ	line
գիշեր	night
գին	price
գինով	drunk
գիտակից	conscious
գիտակցութիւն	consciousness
գիտնալ	to know
գիտութիւն	science
գիտուն	savant
գիր	letter
գիրք	book
գիւղ	village
գիւղացի	peasant
գիւտ	invention
գլխագիր	capital (letter)
գլխարկ	hat
գլխաւոր	chief, principal
գլուխ	head
գծել	to draw
գնահատել	to appreciate
գնահատութիւն	appreciation
գնել	to buy
գոհ	contented

գոհանալ	to give thanks	**Գ**
գոհար	jewel	
գոհունակություն	satisfaction	դանակ — knife
գող	thief	դանդաղ — slow
գոյական	noun, substantive	դաշնագիր — treaty
գոյություն	existence	դաշնակ — piano
գույն	color	դաշնակից — ally
գործ	business, job	դաշնադրություն — treaty
գործադուլ	strike	դաշնակցություն — federation
գործածել	to use	դաշտ — field
գործածություն	use	դառնալ — turn
գործարան	factory	դաս — lesson
գործել	to work	դասագիրք — textbook
գործիք	instrument	դասական — classic
գործողություն	operation	դասատու — teacher
գործօն	active	դասարան — classroom
գոց	closed	դաստիարակ — educator
գոցել	to shut	դաստիարակել — to educate
գութ	pity	դաստիարակու— education
գումար	sum	թիւն
գումարել	to add	դատ — lawsuit
գունավոր	colored	դատարան — court, tribunal
գուշակել	to predict	դատավոր — judge
գուշակություն	prediction	դատել — to judge
գոչել	to exclaim	դատողություն — judgment
գորով	affection	դար — century
գռեհիկ	vulgar	դարձ — return
գտնել	to find	դարձի գալ — to be converted
գրագէտ	writer	դարման — cure
գրականություն	literature	դարմանել — to cure
գրատուն	bookstore	դգալ — spoon
գրավաճառ	bookseller	դեռ — yet
գրգռել	to irritate, provoke	դեռատի — young
գրեթէ	almost	դեսպան — ambassador
գրել	to write	դեսպանատուն — embassy
գրիչ	pen	դերասան — actor
գրկել	to embrace	դերձակ — tailor
գօտի	belt	դէմ — against

դէմք	face
դժբախտ	unfortunate, unhappy
դժբախտաբար	unfortunately
դժբախտութիւն	misfortune
դժոխային	infernal
դժոխք	hell
դժուար	difficult
դիակ	corpse
դիմադրել	to resist
դիմանկար	portrait
դիմաց	opposite
դիտել	to observe
դիտմամբ	intentionally
դիտողութիւն	observation
դիրք	position
դիւանագէտ	diplomat
դիւանագիտական	diplomatic
դիւրին	easy
դիւրութիւն	facility
դնել	to put, to place
դողալ	to tremble
դուն	you, (sing.)
դուռ	door, gate
դուրս	out, outside
դուք	you
դպչել	to touch
դպրոց	school
դրամ	money
դրամատուն	bank
դրացի	neighbor
դրօշ	flag

Ե

եզ	ox
եզակի	singular
եզերք	edge, border, shore
եթէ	if
եթէ ոչ	if not
ելլել	to rise
ելակ	strawberry
ելք	issue, exodus
եկամուտ	income
եկեղեցի	church
եկեղեցական	clergyman
եղանակ	season, tune
եղերական	tragic
եղերերգ	elegy
ենթակայ	subject
եռանդ	ardor
եռանկիւն	triangle
եռամսեայ	trimestrial, quarterly
եռալ, եռացնել	to boil
ես	I
եսասէր	selfish
ետ	back
ետեւ	behind
ետք	after
երազ	dream
երախտագէտ	grateful
երակ	vein
երբ	when
երբեմն	sometimes
երբեք	never
երգ	song
երգել	to sing
երգիչ	singer
երեքշաբթի	Tuesday
երեւալ	to appear
երեւակայել	to imagine
երեւելի	eminent
երէկ	yesterday
երթալ	to go
երթեւեկ	traffic

երիտասարդ	young
երկ	work (literary)
երկաթ	iron
երկաթագործ	blacksmith
երկաթուղի	railroad
երկայն	long
երկինք	sky, heaven
երկիր	earth
երկու	two
երկուշաբթի	Monday
երջանիկ	happy
եւ	and
եւս	also, more

զինուոր	soldier
զինուորական	military
զոհ	victim
զոհողութիւն	sacrifice
զոյգ	pair
զուարթ	gay
զուարճալի	amusing
զուարճութիւն	amusement
զուգահեռական	parallel
զուտ	pure
զուր	in vain
զրկըւ	deprived of
զրկել	to deprive
զօրավար	general (of army)

Զ

զանազան	various
զարդ	ornament
զարդարել	to adorn
զարմանք	wonder
զարմանալի	wonderful
զարմանալիօրէն	wonderfully
զարնել	to hit
զաւակ	child
զգացում	sentiment
զգեստ	clothing
զգոյշ	careful
զգուշանալ	to be careful
զգուշութիւն	care
զեղուն	overflowing
զեռուն	reptile
զետեղել	to place, situate
զերծ	free of
զզուիլ	to be disgusted
զէնք	arms
զինադադար	armistice

Է

էակ	being
էական	essential
էապէս	essentially
էութիւն	being, essence
էգ	female
էշ	donkey
էջ	page

Ը

ըլլալ	to be
ընդարձակ	vast
ընդարձակել	to enlarge
ընդհակառակն	on the contrary
ընդհանուր	general
ընդունելարան	receptacle
ընդունիլ	to accept

ընդվզել	to revolt
ընել	to do
ընկեր	companion
ընկերանալ	to accompany
ընկերություն	company
ընկույզ	walnut
ըսել	to say
ընտանի	domestic
ընտանիք	family
ընտրանի	elite
ընտրել	to choose
ընտրություն	choice, election

Թ

թագ	crown
թագավոր	king
թագավորական	royal
թագավորություն	kingdom
թաթ	paw
թակարդ	trap
թաղել	to bury
թանձր	thick, dense
թատերախաղ	play (theater)
թատրոն	theater
թարգման	translator
թարգմանել	to translate
թաց	wet
թավիշ	velvet
թեկնածու	candidate
թերևս	perhaps
թերի	defective
թերություն	defect
թև	wing, arm
թէ	that
թէյ	tea
թթու	acid
թի	oar

թիւ	number
թղթաբեր	mail (incoming)
թղթատար	mail (outgoing)
թղթակից	correspondent
թղթակցություն	correspondence
թշնամի	enemy
թողուլ	to leave
թոյն	poison
թուական	date
թուանշան	figure (arith.)
թուզ	fig
թուղթ	paper
թունաւոր	poisonous
թունաւորել	to poison
թուշ	chin
թուփ	bush
թռչիլ	to fly
թռչուն	bird

Ժ

ժամ	hour
ժամանակ	time
ժամանակակից	contemporary
ժամանակացոյց	time table
ժամանակաւոր	temporary
ժամացոյց	watch, clock
ժայռ	rock
ժապաւէն	ribbon
ժառանգ, ժառանգորդ	heir
ժառանգություն	inheritance, legacy
ժիր	diligent
ժլատ	stingy
ժխտական	negative
ժխտել	to negate

ժողով	meeting	ի վեր	since
ժողովուրդ	people	իր	his (pronoun); object
ժողովրդական	popular		
ժուժկալ	sober	իրագործել	to realize
ժպիտ	smile	իրական	real
ժպտիլ	to smile	իրապէս	really
		իրաւ	true
		իրաւագէտ	jurist
		իրաւունք	right
ի		իրաւարախ	arbiter
		իրիկուն	evening
		իրողութիւն	fact
իբր, իբրև	as	իւղ	oil
իբր թէ	if	իւրաքանչիւր	each
իգական	feminine		
իժ	viper		
իմ	my		
իմինս	mine	**Լ**	
իմանալ	to hear		
իմաստ	sense		
իմաստասէր	philosopher	լալ	to weep
իմաստութիւն	wisdom	լայն	wide
իմաստուն	wise	լապտեր	lantern
իմացական	intellectual	լաստ	raft
իյնալ	to fall	լար	chord
ինը	nine	լաց	weeping
իննսուն	ninety	լաւ	good, well
ինչ	what	լաւագոյն	better
ինչպէս	how	լաւատես	optimist
ինչու	why	լեարդ	liver
ինք	he	լեզու	tongue, language
ինքնաբուխ	spontaneous	լեղի	bitter
ինքնաթիռ	jet	լեռ	mountain
ինքնակալ	autocrat	լեռնային	mountainous
ինքնատիպ	original	լեցնել	to fill
ինքնութիւն	identity	լի	full
իշխան	prince	լիճ	lake
իսկ	but, and	լճակ	small lake
իսկապէս	essentially	լման	entire, complete

170

լմնցնել	to finish
լոգարան	bathroom
լողանալ	to bathe
լույս	light
լուռ	silent
լուսապսակ	halo
¹լուսավոր	luminous, luminary
լուսավորիչ	illuminator
լուր	news
լուրջ	serious
լռել	to keep silence
լսել	to hear
լսողություն	hearing
լրագիր	newspaper
լրտես	spy

խ

խաբեբայ	cheater
խաբել	to cheat, to fool
խածնել	to bite
խակ	raw, immature
խաղ	play
խաղալ	to play
խաղաղ	quiet, peaceful
խաղաղություն	peace
խաղող	grape
խայթ	bite
(խիղճ խայթ)	scruples
խայթել	to sting
խայծ	bait
խանդ	ardor
խանդավառ	enthusiastic
խանդավառություն	enthusiasm
խանութ	shop

խաչ	cross
խաչել	to crucify
խառն	mixed
խառնել	to mix
խառնուրդ	mixture
խավար	dark, darkness
խավարում	eclipse
խելացի	intelligent
խելք	intelligence
խեղճ	poor
խեղճություն	poverty
խենթ	crazy
խիզախ	audacious
խիղճ	conscience
խիստ	severe, very
խիտ	dense
խղճալ	to pity
խղճալի	pitiable, pitiful
խղճամիտ	conscientious
խղճահարվել	to have scruples, to repent
խմել	to drink
խնամել	to take care of
խնայել	to economize, save
խնայողություն	saving
խնդիր	problem
խնդրանք	request
խնդրել	to request
խոկալ	to meditate
խոհ	thought
խոնարհ	humble
խոնավ	damp
խոստովանել	to confess
խոր , խորունկ	deep
խորհուրդ	mystery, thought
խորհրդածել	meditate
խորհրդակցել	to consult
խորհրդարան	parliament

խորտակել	to destroy
խուլ	deaf
խումբ	group
խուսափիլ	to avoid
խրատ	advice
խրատել	to give advice
խրախճութիւն	convention
խօսիլ	to speak
խօսք	word

Ծ

ծագիլ	to originate
ծագում	origin
ծալել	to fold
ծալք	fold
ծախել	to sell
ծախք	expense
ծածանիլ	to float
ծածկել	to cover
ծածուկ	hidden
ծակ	hole
ծակել	to pierce
ծաղիկ	flower
ծաղկաքաղ	anthology
ծաղր	mockery
ծաղրել	to mock
ծամել	to chew
ծայր	extremity
ծանր	heavy
ծառ	tree
ծարաւ	thirst, thirsty
ծափ	clap
ծեծ	thrashing
ծեծել	to thrash
ծերակոյտ	senate
ծերակուտական	senator

ծիածան	rainbow
ծիլ	bud
ծիծաղ	laughter
ծիլել	to bud
ծիրան	apricot
ծիրանի գօտի	rainbow
ծխալ	to fume
ծխել	to smoke
ծնիլ	to be born
ծնողք	parents
ծնունդ	birth
ծոյլ	lazy
ծուղակ	snare
ծուռ	crooked
ծռել	to bend
ծրար	package, bundle
ծփալ	to float
ծփուն	afloat

Կ

կազմել	to form
կազմակերպել	to organize
կաթ	milk
կաթիլ	drop
կաթողիկէ	cathedral
կալուած	property, domain
կախարդ	sorcerer, witch
կախարդային	bewitching, enchanting
կաղ	lame
կաղալ	to limp
կաղանդ	new year
կամ	or
կամար	arch
կամաւոր	voluntary, volunteer
կամուրջ	bridge

կամք	will, will power
կայարան	station
կայուն —ություն	stable, stability
կայծ	sparkle
կայծակ	lightning
կայմ	mast
կանգնիլ	to stand up
կայսր	emperor
կայսերական	imperial
կայսերապաշտ	imperialist
կայտառ	robust
կանանչ	green
կանացի	womanly
կանգնիլ	to stand up
կանգուն	standing
կանթեղ	lamp
կանխել	to anticipate
կանխիկ	cash
կանոն	rule
կանոնաւոր	regular
կանուխ	early
կանչել	to call
կաշառել	to bribe
կաշառք	bribe
կապ	tie
կապակցութիւն	connection
կապել	to tie, bind
կապիկ	monkey
կապկել	to imitate
կապոյտ	blue
կառախումբ	train
կառավար	coachman
կառավարական	governmental
կառավարել	to govern
կառավարիչ	governor
կառավարութիւն	government
կառուցանել	to construct
կառք	carriage, cab
կատաղի	furious
կատարեալ	perfect
կատարել	to perform
կատարելութիւն	perfection
կատարելապէս	perfectly
կատու	cat
կար	sewing
կարագ	butter
կարասի	furniture
կարգ	class
կարդալ	to read
կարել	to sew
կարելի	possible
կարելիութիւն	possibility
կարենալ	to be able
կարեկցիլ	to sympathize
կարեկցութիւն	sympathy
կարեւոր	important
կարեւորութիւն	importance
կարծիք	opinion
կարծր	hard
կարծրանալ	to harden
կարճ	short
կարմիր	red
կարող	able, capable
կարոտ	needy
կարօտ	nostalgia
կաւիճ	chalk
կեանք	life
կեղեւ	bark (of tree)
կեղծ	false
կեղծաւոր	hypocrite
կեղծիք	sham
կեղտ	dirt
կեղտոտ	dirty
կենդանի	animal, alive
կենսական	vital
կենսանիւթ	vitamin

173

կեռաս	cherry	կրոնական	religious
կերակուր	food	կրոնաւոր	clergyman
կերպ	manner	կրոնք	religion
կէտ	point, whale		
կզակ	jaw		
կը	particle used in indicative present and imperfect tenses	**Հ**	
կին	woman	հագուստ	clothing
կիրակի	Sunday	հագնիլ	to put on, to dress
կիրք	passion	հագուիլ	to get dressed
կից	kick, abutting	հազ	cough
կլիմայ	climate	հազալ	to cough
կլլել	to swallow	հազիւ	hardly, scarcely
կղերական	clergyman	հազուագիւտ	rare
կղզի	island	հալածանք	persecution
կմախք	skeleton	հալածել	to persecute
կնճռոտ	complicated	հալեցնել	to melt (tr.)
կշիռ	balance, weight	հալիլ	to melt (intr.)
կողմ	side	հականիշ	antonym
կողք	cover (of book)	հակառակ	contrary, in spite of
կոչել	to call		
կոր	curved	հակառակորդ	adversary
կորիզ	nucleus	հաճելի	agreeable
կորիզային	nuclear	հաճիլ	to please
կորանցնել	to lose	հաճոյք	pleasure
կործանել	to ruin	համ	taste, savor
կուռք	idol	համաձայնիլ	to agree with
կուրծք	breast	համար	for
կռապաշտութիւն	idolatry	համարձակ	bold
		համարձակիլ	to dare
կռուիլ	to fight	համբոյր	kiss
կտակ	testament	համբուրել	to kiss
կտոր	piece	համեղ	tasty
կտուց	beak, bill	համեմատ	according
կրակ	fire	հայ	Armenian (n. & adj.)
կրակապաշտութիւն	fire worship		
		հայաստան	Armenia
կրտսեր	younger	հայերէն	Armenian (lang.)

174

Հայկական	Armenian	Հատ	piece
Հայր	father	Հատիկ	grain
Հայրական	paternal	Հատնիլ	to expire, run out
Հայրենակից	compatriot	Հատուած	segment
Հայրենասէր	patriot	Հարազատ	pure, unadulterated
Հայրենասիրական	patriotic	Հարազատութիւն	purity, genuineness
Հայրենասիրու-թիւն	patriotism	Հարաւ	south
		Հարաւային	southern
Հայրենիք	fatherland	Հարուած	blow
Հայրութիւն	fatherhood, paternity	Հարուածել	hit, strike
		Հարուստ	rich
Հանգրուան	milestone	Հարս	bride
Հանգիստ	rest	Հարսանիք	wedding
Հանգչիլ	to rest	Հարցնել	to ask
Հանգստաւէտ	comfortable	Հարցում	question
Հանդէպ	toward	Հաց	bread
Հանդիսա	spectacle	Հաւ	hen
Հանդիսատես	spectator	Հաւանական	probable
Հանդիսաւոր	spectacular, solemn	Հաւանութիւն	approval
Հանճար	genius	Հաւանիլ	to assent
Հանճարեղ	with genius	Հաւասար	equal
Հաշիւ	account	Հաւասարապէս	equally
Հաշուակալ	accountant	Հաւատալ	to believe
Հաշտեցնել	to reconcile	Հաւատարիմ	faithful
Հաշտութիւն	peace, reconciliation	Հաւատք	faith
		Հաւաքաբար	collectively
Հաչել	to bark	Հաւաքածոյ	collection
Հապճեպ	hasty	Հաւաքել	to collect, gather
Հասարակ	common	Հաւաքոյթ	gathering
Հասարակութիւն	public (n.)	Հաւաքուիլ	assemble
Հասկ	ear of corn, wheat	Հաւնիլ	to like, approve
Հասկնալ	to understand	Հեգնանք	irony
Հասկացողութիւն	understanding	Հեգնել	to ridicule, to deride
Հասնիլ	to arrive	Հեզ	meek
Հասոյթ	income	Հեթանոս	pagan
Հաստ	thick	Հեթանոսութիւն	paganism
Հաստատ	solid	Հեռաւոր	distant
Հասողութիւն	reach	Հեռու	far

175

հետ	with	հովանոց	umbrella
հետաքրքիր	curious	հովիւ	shepherd
հետեւանք	consequence	հոտ	smell
հետեւիլ	to follow	հուն	there
զոր	mighty	հոտիլ	to smell (intr.)
հիանալ	to admire	հոտոտել, հոտ-	to smell
հիանալի	admirable	ւըրալ	
հիացում	admiration	հում	raw
հիմ	foundation, base	հունձք	harvest
հիմնական	fundamental, basic	հպիլ	to touch
հիմնարկ	foundation, institu-	հսկայ	giant
	tion	հսկել	to watch
հին	old	հրաժարական	resignation
հինգշաբթի	Thursday	հրաժարիլ	to resign
հիւանդ	sick	հրահանգ	exercise
հիւանդանալ	to get sick	հրահանգել	to instruct
հիւանդանոց	hospital	հրայրք	passion
հիւլէ, հիւլէական	atom, atomic	հրաշալի	miraculous
հիւպատոս	consul	հրաշք	miracle
հիւսիս	north	հրապարակ	market
հիւր	guest	հրապոյր	charm
հիւրասէր	hospitable	հրապուրել	to charm, enchant
հիւրասիրութիւն	hospitality	հրապուրիչ	charming
հնազանդ	obedient	հրատարակել	to publish
հնարել	to invent	հրատարակիչ	publisher
հնարիչ	inventor	հրաւէր	invitation
հնարք	invention	հրաւիրել	to invite
հնձել	to reap	հրդեհ	fire
հոգ	care	հրել	to push
հոգալ	to care, provide	հրճուանք	joy
հոգի	soul		
հոգեկան	spiritual		
հոմանիշ	synonym		
հոն	there		**Ձ**
հոս	here		
հոսանք	current	ձայն	sound, voice
հոսիլ	to flow	ձայնական	vocal
հով	wind	ձայնասփիւռ	radio

176

ձայնասփռել	to broadcast
ձայնաւոր	vowel
ձանձրանալ	to be bored
ձանձրոյթ	boredom, ennui
ձեղուն	ceiling
ձեռնական	manual
ձեռնադրել	to ordain
ձեռնարկ	enterprise
ձեռնարկել	to undertake
ձեռք	hand
ձեր	your
ձիրք	gift
ձիւն	snow
ձմեռ	winter
ձմերուկ	watermelon

Ղ

ղեկ	helm
ղեկավար	helmsman, leader
ղեկավարել	to conduct, direct
ղրկել	to send

Ճ

ճագար	rabbit
ճաթել	to burst
ճախրել	to soar
ճակատ	forehead, front
ճակատագիր	fate
ճակատագրական	fateful
ճակատամարտ	battle
ճամբայ	way
ճամբորդել	to travel
ճամբորդութիւն	travel, journey
ճանճ	fly (insect)
ճանչնալ	to know, recognize

ճաշ	meal
ճառ	speech
ճառագայթ	ray
ճառել	to deliver a speech
ճիշդ	correct, exact
ճիւաղ	monster
ճիւաղային	monstrous
ճմլել	to press
ճնճղուկ	sparrow
ճշդել	to correct
ճշդութիւն	exactitude
ճշմարիտ	true
ճշմարտապէս	truly

Մ

մագնիս	magnet
մագնիսական	magnetic
մազ	hair
մակարդակ	plane, level (n.)
մակբայ	adverb
մակերես	surface
մահ	death
մահացու	fatal
մայր	mother
մանաւանդ	above all, especially
մանկական	childish
մանկութիւն	childhood
մանուկ	child
մանր	tiny
մաշիլ	to get worn
մաս	part
մասնագէտ	specialist
մասնակի	partial
մասնաւոր	special
մասնաւորաբար	especially
մատ	finger

մատանի	ring	մեր	our
մատիտ	pencil	մերժել	to refuse
մատնել	to betray	մերկ	naked
մարգ, մարգա-գետին	meadow	մերկացնել	to lay bare
մարգարէ	prophet	մէգ	fog
մարգարիտ	pearl	մէկ	one
մարդ	man	մէջ	in
մարդակազմու-թիւն	anatomy	մէջէն	through
մարդկային	human	մը	a, an
մարդկութիւն	humanity	մթնոլորտ	atmosphere
մարզիկ	athlete	մժեղ	mosquito
մարմին	body	մի	one
մարմնամարզ	gymnastics	միայն	only
մարմնաւոր	bodily, corporeal	միացեալ	united
մաքուր	clean	միացեալ նա-հանգներ	United States
մաքրել	to clean	միասին	together
մելան	ink	միաւոր	unit
մեծ	great, big	միայնակ	alone
մեկնակէտ	starting point	մինչ, մինչդեռ	while
մեկնել	to interpret	մինչեւ	until, as far as
մեկնութիւն	interpretation	միշտ	always
մեկնիլ	to depart	միջակ	mediocre
մեկնում	departure	միջուկ	kernel
մեղանչել	to sin	միս	flesh, meat
մեղաւոր	sinful	մնալ	to remain
մեղմ	mild	մոլեռանդ	fanatic
մեղր	honey	մոլի	addict
մեղք	sin	մոլոր	wandering, gone astray
մենաւոր	solitary	մոլորակ	planet
մենութիւն	solitude	մոլութիւն	vice
մենք	we	մոմ	candle
մեռեալ	dead	մութ	dark
մեռնիլ	to die	մսավաճառ	butcher
մեռցնել	to kill	մսխել	to waste, squander
մետաղ	metal	մսխում	waste
մետաղեայ	metallic	մտահոգ	worried

178

մտերիմ	intimate
մտնել	**to enter**
մրմնջել	to murmur
մրմունջ	murmur
մրցակից	competitor
մրցիլ	to compete
մրցում	competition, rivalry

Յ

յաճախ	often
յաղթական	victorious
յաղթանակ	victory
յաղթութիւն	triumph
յայտնի	evident
յայտնութիւն	revelation
յանդգնութիւն	boldness
յանդուգն	bold
յանկարծ	suddenly
յանկարծակի	sudden
յանցաւոր	guilty
յանցանք	guilt
յաջող	successful
յաջողիլ	to succeed
յաջողապէս	successfully
յաջորդ	next
յաջորդաբար	successively
յաջորդական	successive
յաջորդութիւն	succession
յառաջ	forward
յառաջդիմութիւն	progress
յատակ	bottom, background
յատկութիւն	quality
յատուկ	proper
յարաբերական	relative
յարաբերութիւն	relation
յարգանք	respect
յարգել	to respect

յարկ	floor, story, **home**
յարձակում	attack
յարձակողական	aggressive
յաւիտեան	for ever
յաւիտենական	eternal
յեղափոխական	revolutionist
յեղափոխութիւն	revolution
յիմար	fool
յիշատակ	souvenir
յիշել	to remember
յիշողութիւն	memory
յոգնակի	plural
յոգնած	tired
յոգնիլ	to get tired
յոյս	hope
յորդիլ	to overflow
յուսալ	to hope
յուսախաբ	disappointed
յուսախաբութիւն	disappointment
յստակ	clear
յօրինել	to compose

Ն

նաեւ	also
նախ	at first
նախագահ	president
նախապէս	originally, **previously, formerly**
նախարար	minister
նախդիր, նախադրութիւն	preposition
նախընտրել	to prefer
նախկին	former
նախնիք	ancestor
նահատակ	martyr
նահանգ	state, **province**
նամակ	letter
նայիլ	to look

նաւ	vessel
նաւակ	bark
նաւել	to navigate
նեղ	narrow
նեղուց	strait
ներկ	color, paint
ներկայ	present
ներկայացնել	to introduce
ներկել	to paint
ներկարար	painter
ներշնչել	to inspire
ներշնչում	inspiration
ներս	into, inside
ներփակ	enclosed
ներփակել	to enclose
նիհար	thin
նիհարնալ	to get thin
նկար	painting
նկարագիր	character
նկարագրել	to describe
նկարել	to paint
նկարիչ	painter (artist)
նման	like, similar
նշան	sign
նշանակել	to signify
նոր	new
նուէր	present, gift
նուիրել	to present
նուիրական	sacred
նուիրում	dedication
նստիլ	to sit

Շ

շաբաթ	week
շաբաթ օր	Saturday
շաբաթավերջ	weekend

շահ	profit
շահիլ	to earn, to gain
շաղկապ	conjunction
շատ	much
շարժել	to move (tr.)
շարժիլ	to move (intr.)
շարժական	movable
շարժանկար	movies
շարժում	movement
շարունակ	continually
շարունակել	to continue
շաքար	sugar
շաքարեղէն	candies
շեղ	oblique, slanting
շեղակի	obliquely
շեղիլ	to deviate
շեղում	deviation
շեշտ	accent
շեշտել	to accentuate
շերտ	slice
շէն	thriving, prosperous
շինական	peasant
շինարար	constructive
շինել	to build
շիտակ	straight
շնորհ	grace
շնորհիւ	thanks to
շնչել	to breathe
շնչերակ	artery
շշուկ	whisper
շոգենաւ	steamer
շոգի	steam
շուարիլ	to get confused
շուն	dog
շունչ	breath
շուտ	quick
շուրջ	around, about
շրջան	period, era, tour

շրջանակ	frame, circumference
շրջապատ	environment
շրջապատել	to surround
շփել	to rub
շփում	friction
շփոթել	to confuse
շփոթել	to be confused
շփոթություն	confusion

II

ոեւէ	any
ողբալ	to lament
ողբերգություն	tragedy
ողջ	alive
ողորկ	smooth
ոճ	style
ոճիր	crime
ոճրագործ	criminal
ոմանք	some
ոմն	some one
ոչ	no
ոչինչ	nothing
ով	who
ոստում	jump
ոստրէ	oyster
ոտանավոր	poem
ոտք	foot
որ	who, which
որբ	orphan
որբանոց	orphanage
որդեգրել	adopt
որեւէ	any
որեւիցէ	any

որոշ	definite
որոշել	to decide
որոշում	decision
որովհետեւ	because
որքան	how much
որջ	den
որպէսզի	so that
որոտալ	to thunder
որսալ	to hunt
որսորդ	hunter
ուզել	to wish, to want
ութ	eight
ութսուն	eighty
ուժ	force
ուժեղ	strong
ուլ	kid
ուղիղ	straight
ուղղակի	direct
ուղղել	to correct
ուղղություն	direction
ուղտ	camel
ունայն	vain
ունենալ	to have
ունկնդիր	listener
ունկնդրել	to listen
ուշ	late
ուշանալ	to be late
ուռենալ	to swell
ուռեցք	swelling
ուռիլ	to swell
ուսուցիչ	teacher
ուտել	to eat
ուտելիք	eatable, food
ուր	where
ուրուագիծ	outline
ուրուագծել	to outline
ուրուանկար	silhouette
ուրեմն	therefore
ուրիշ	other

Ջ

չակերտ	quotation mark
չամիչ	raisin
չար	bad, naughty
չարագործ	malefactor
չարիք	evil
չարախօսել	to slander, backbite
չարամիտ	malicious
չարչարել	to torture
չափազանց	too much, extremely
չափաւոր	moderate
չեզոք	neutral
չնչին	insignificant
չոր	dry
չորս	four
չորքոտանի	four footed
չուան	rope
չմշկել	to skate
չթմբեանք	excuse, justification
չքնաղ	lovely

Պ

պակաս	minus, lacking
պակասաւոր	defective
պահ	moment
պահակ	sentinel
պահանջ	demand, claim
պահապան	guardian
պահանջատէր	creditor
պահանջել	to demand
պահարան	closet, envelope
պահել	to keep
պահք	fasting, lenten
պաղ	cold
պաղատանք	entreaty
պաղատիլ	to beseech
պաղեցնել	make cold
պաղպաղակ	ice cream
պայթիլ	to explode
պայթիւն, պայթում	explosion
պայծառ	clear
պայման	condition
պայմանագրութիւն	contract
պայմանադրական	conventional
պայմանաւոր	conditional
պայուսակ	bag
պայքար	struggle
պանդոկ	hotel
պանդոկապետ	inn keeper
պանիր	cheese
պանծալ	to take pride
պանծալի	magnificent
պանծացնել	to magnify
պաշար	supplies, provision
պաշարել	to besiege
պաշտամունք	worship
պաշտել	to worship, adore
պաշտելի	adorable
պաշտում	adoration
պաշտպան	protector
պաշտպանել	to protect
պաշտօն	office
պաշտօնական	official (adj.)
պաշտօնատար	functionary official (n.)
պաշտօնեայ	employee
պապ, պապիկ	grandpa
պապակ	thirst
պառաւ	old woman
պատ	wall
պատահար	incident
պատկառելի	venerable

պապադայ	case, circumstance
պարզ	simple
պարզել	to simplify
պարզապէս	simply
պարիկ	fairy
պարծենալ	to boast
պարկ	sack, bag
պարկեշտ	honest
պարոն	sir, gentlman, Mr.
պարել	to dance
պարուհի	danseuse
պարունակել	to contain
պարունակութիւն	contents
պատրուակ	pretext
պարպել	to empty, evacuate
պարսաւել	to blame
պարսիկ	Persian
պարսկերէն	Persian (language)
պարտական	debtor
պարտականու-	duty
թիւն	
պարտատէր	debtor
պարտաւոր ըլլալ	to be obliged
պարտաւորիչ	obligatory
պարտէզ	garden
պարտիզպան	gardener
պարտութիւն	defeat
պարտուիլ	to be defeated
պարտք	debt
պարփակել	to encompass
պեխ	moustache
պեղել	to dig
պետ	chief
պետական	governmental
պետութիւն	state
պերճ	luxurious
պերճախօս	eloquent
պզտիկ	small
պէս	like, similar

պէսպէս	of various kinds, varied
պէտք	necessity
պէտք է որ	it is necessary that
պժգալ	to loathe
պժգալի	disgusting
պինդ	firm, hard
պիսակ	beauty spot
պիստակ	pistachio
պիտակ	label
պիտանի	useful
պիտի	particle for future tense
պղինձ	copper
պղպջակ	bubble
պճնել	adorn
պնակ	dish, plate
պողոտայ	avenue
պսակ	wreath, marriage
պսակել	to crown
պտուղ	fruit
պտղալի	fruitful

Ջ

ջարդ	massacre
ջարդել	to massacre
ջերմ	warm
ջինջ	clear
ջնջել	wipe out
ջուր	water

Ռ

ռահվիրայ	pioneer
ռամիկ	vulgar
ռամկավարութիւն	democracy
ռամկավար	democrat

Ս

սա	this
սագ	goose
սաթ	amber
սալ	anvil
սակարկել	to bargain
սահիլ	to slide
սահման	limit, frontier
սահմանադրու–թիւն	constitution
սահմանադրական	constitutional
սահմանակից	bordering
սառ	ice
սառնարան	icebox
սառուցիկ	freezing
սարսափ	terror
սաւան	sheet
սաւառնիլ	to soar
սափրիչ	barber
սեխ	melon
սեղան	table
սեղանատուն	dining room
սեղմել	to press
սեմ	threshold
սեռ	sex
սերտել	to study
սէր	love
սին	vain
սիրական	darling
սիրահար	lover
սիրահարիլ	to fall in love
սիրել	to love
սիրերգ	love song
սիրուն	lovely
սիրտ	heart
սխալ	error, mistake
սխալիլ	to be mistaken
սկիզբ	beginning

սկզբունք	principle
սկսիլ	to begin
սկսնակ	beginner
սողալ	to creep
սողուն	reptile
սովորական	ordinary, customary
սովորութիւն	custom, habit
սուղ	expensive
սուրբ	saint
ստանալ	to receive
ստանձնել	to undertake
ստուգել	to verify, ascertain

Վ

վազել	to run
վախ	fear
վախկոտ	timid
վախնալ	to fear
վայրենի	savage
վայրի	wild
վանական	monk (n.) monastic (adj.)
վանել	to chase, dispel
վանք	monastery, convent
վառարան	stove
վատ	coward
վատնել	to waste
վատնում	waste
վար	below, down
վարանել	to hesitate
վարանում	hesitation
վարդ	rose
վարել	to conduct, to drive (car)
վարժուիլ	to get accustomed
վարժութիւն	practice, training

վարձատրել	to reward
վարձատրութիւն	reward
վարձել	to rent
վարձք	rent
վեր	up
վերաքաղ	recapitulation
վերմակ	blanket
վերջ	end
վերջակէտ	period
վերջանալ	to end (intr.)
վերջացնել	to finish
վերջաւորութիւն	end
վէրք	wound
վիճակ	state, condition
վիրաբոյժ	surgeon
վիրաւոր	wounded
վիրաւորել	to wound, injure, offend
վկայ	witness
վկայական	certificate
վկայել	to witness
վհատ	desperate
վհատիլ	to despair
վճիռ	judgment, sentence
վճռել	to decree, decide
վռնտել	to expel
վտարել	to turn out, banish, expel
վրայ	on
վրէժ	revenge

S

տալ	to give
տախտակ	wood, plank
տախտակամած	floor
տակ	under
տակառ	barrel
տաղ	ode
տաղանդ	talent
տաղանդաւոր	talented
տաճար	temple
տաղաչափ	versifier
տաղաչափել	to versify
տաղաչափութիւն	versification
տամուկ	damp, wet
տանիլ	to carry, tolerate
տանիք	roof
տանձ	pear
տաշել	to file, shave
տառ	letter
տառացի	literal
տասանորդ	tithe (tax)
տասը	ten
տարբեր	different
տարբերութիւն	difference
տարեկան	yearly
տարի	year
տարտամ	vague
տափակ	flat
տաք	hot
տգեղ	ugly
տգէտ	ignorant
տեղ	place
տեղական	local
տեսակ	sort, kind
տեսական	theoretical
տեսակցութիւն	interview
տեսանելի	visible
տեսիլք	vision
տեսնել	to see
տեսողական	visual
տեսութիւն	theory
տերեւ	leaf
տեւական	lasting
տեւականացում	perpetuation
տեւել	to last

տեւողութիւն	duration	**փ**	
տէր	owner, Lord		
տիեզերական	universal	փայտ	wood
տիեզերք	universe	փայտակէն	wooden
տիկին	lady, Mrs.	փառասէր	ambitious
տիրանալ	to become the owner, master	փառասիրութիւն	ambition
		փառաւոր	glorious
տխուր	sad	փառք	glory
տղայ	boy, child	փեսայ	bridegroom
տոկոս	interest	փթթիլ	to blossom
տոկուն	solid	փնտռել	to seek, search
տոմարակալ	book-keeper	փոթորիկ	storm
տոմարակալու-	book-keeping	փորձ	trial, essay
թիւն		փորձել	to try
տուն	house, home	փունջ	bouquet
տուրք	tax, tribute	փուռ	oven
տուփ	box	փտտիլ	to rot
		փրթիլ	to break off (intr.)
		փրկարար	salutary
ր		փրկել	to save
		փրկիչ	savior
րաբունի	rabbi	փրկութիւն	salvation
րոպէ	second, moment		

ց		**ք**	
ցամաք	land (n.) dry (adj.)	քալել	to walk
ցանել	to sow	քակել	to undo
ցանցառ	sparse	քահանայ	priest
ցասում	wrath	քաղաք	city
ցաւ	pain	քաղաքական	political
ցաւալի	regrettable	քաղաքականու-	politics
ցեղ	race	թիւն	
ցեղային	racial	քաղաքացի	citizen
ցոյց	demonstration	քաղել	to cull, gather
ցուցահանդէս	fair	քաղցր	sweet
ցուցարար	demonstrator	քամել	press, squeeze
ցուցնել	to show	քան	than
		քանդակ	sculpture

186

քանդակագործ	sculptor	օգնութիւն	help
քանի	how many	օգոստոս	August
քաջ	courageous	օգտակար	useful
քաջագործութիւն	deeds of valor	օդ	air
քաջութիւն	courage	օդային	aerial
քերականութիւն	grammar	օդանաւ	airship, airplane
քէն	grudge	օդանաւորդ	aviator
քինախնդիր	vindictive	օդուժ	air force
քիչ	little (quantity)	օժանդակ	auxiliary
քմայք	caprice	օժանդակել	to help
քմայքոտ	capricious	օծել	anoint
քնանալ	to sleep	օձ	snake
քնար	lyre	օձիք	collar
քնարերգակ	lyric	օղ	ear-ring
քննադատ	critic	օղակ	link
քննադատել	to criticize	օր	day
քշել	to drive	օրական	daily, daily salary
քոյր	sister	օրաթերթ	daily newspaper
քով	near	օրէնսդիր	legislative
քուն	sleep	օրէնք	law
քսան	twenty	օրինական	legal, legitimate
		օրիորդ	Miss, young lady
		օրհնել	to bless
		օրհնութիւն	blessing

O

օգնական	assistant
օգնել	to help

ENGLISH - ARMENIAN

A

English	Armenian
a, an	*մը*
abdomen	*որովայն, փոր*
able	*կարող*
about	*շուրջ, մասին*
absence	*բացակայություն*
absent	*բացակայ*
absolute	*բացարձակ*
absurd	*անհեթեթ*
abundance	*առատություն*
abundant	*առատ*
accept	*ընդունիլ*
accident	*արկած*
accompany	*ընկերանալ*
according	*համաձայն*
accordingly	*հետեւաբար*
account	*հաշիւ*
accumulate	*կուտակել*
accurate	*ճիշդ, ուղիղ*
accuse	*ամբաստանել*
acid	*թթու*
across	*մէջէն*
act	*գործ, արար թա- տերախաղի*
active	*գործօն*
activity	*գործունէություն*
actor	*դերասան*
add	*գումարել, աւել- ցընել*
addition	*գումար*
address	*հասցէ*
adjust	*յարմարցնել, ուղղել*

English	Armenian
admire	*հիանալ*
advertisement	*ազդ*
aerial	*օդային*
afraid	*վախցած*
after	*խող*
again	*դարձեալ*
against	*դէմ*
age	*տարիք*
ago	*առաջ*
agree	*համաձայնիլ*
agreement	*համաձայնություն*
aid	*օգնություն*
air	*օդ*
air force	*օդուժ*
all	*բոլոր*
allow	*թոյլատրել*
aloud	*բարձրաձայն*
almost	*գրեթէ*
already	*արդէն*
although	*թէեւ, թէպէտ*
always	*միշտ*
among	*մէջ*
amount	*գումար*
amuse	*զուարճացնել*
amusement	*զուարճություն*
and	*եւ*
angel	*հրեշտակ*
anger	*բարկություն*
angle	*անկիւն*
angry	*բարկացած*
animal	*կենդանի*
another	*ուրիշ մը*
answer	*պատասխան*
ant	*մրջիւն*

188

any	որևէ, ոևէ	astonish	զարմացնել
appear	երևալ	astronaut	աստղանաւորդ
appearance	երևոյթ	astronomer	աստղագէտ
appetite	ախորժակ	astronomy	աստղագիտու–
apple	խնձոր		թիւն
apply	դիմել, դնել	at	մէջ
appreciate	գնահատել	atmosphere	մթնոլորտ
appreciation	գնահատություն	atom	հիւլէ
approach (n.)	մօտեցում	atomic	հիւլէական
approach (v.)	մօտենալ	attach	կապկնել
approval	հաւանություն	attack	յարձակիլ
apt	յարմար	attempt	փորձել
arbitrary	կամայական	attention	ուշադրություն
arc	աղեղ	attest	վկայել
arch	կամար	attraction	ձգողություն
area	տարածություն	attractive	գրաւիչ
arise	ելլել	attribute	վերագրել
arithmetic	թուաբանություն	aunt	հօրաքոյր, մօ–
ark	տապան		րաքյր
arm	բազուկ, դ:նք	author	հեղինակ
army	բանակ	authority	հեղինակություն
arrange	կարգադրել	automatic	ինքնագործ
arrangement	կարգադրություն	automobile	ինքնաշարժ
arrow	նետ	average	միջին
art	արուեստ	auxiliary	օժանդակ
artery	շնչերակ	awake	արթուն, արթըն–
article	առարկայ, յօդ		ցնել
artisan	արհեստաւոր	away	անդին
artist	արուեստագէտ	awful	սարսափելի
as	մինչ, ինման	awkward	անճարակ
ascribe	վերագրել	axis	առանցք
ash	մոխիր, աճիւն		
ashamed	ամչցած		
ask	հարցնել, խնդրել	B	
ass	էշ		
assemble	հաւաքել	baby	երախայ
assume	ենթադրել	back	կռ, ետև
assure	վստահեցնել	bad	գէշ
assurance	ապահովություն	bag	պայուսակ

189

balance	կշիռ, հաւասարակշռութիւն	black	սեւ
bale	հակ	blade	ծիղ, շեղբի
ball	գնդակ	bless	օրհնել
band	խումբ	blessing	օրհնութիւն
bank	դրամատուն	blind	կոյր
bankrupt	սնանկ	blindness	կուրութիւն
bare	մերկ	blood	արիւն
bark	կեղեւ, հաչել	bloom	բողբոջ, բողբոջել
base	խարխիս, ստորին	blow	փչել, հարուած
basic	հիմնական	blue	կապոյտ
basin	աւազան, կոնք	boast	պարծենալ
basket	զամբիւղ	boat	նաւ
bath	բաղնիք	body	մարմին
be	ըլլալ	boil	եռալ, եռացնել
beak	կտուց	bone	ոսկոր
bear	արջ, կրել	book	գիրք
beard	մօրուք	book-keeping	տոմարակալութիւն
beast	անասուն	boot	մուճակ
beautiful	գեղեցիկ	bottle	շիշ
because	որովհետեւ	box	տուփ
bed	անկողին	boy	մանչ
bee	մեղու	brain	ուղեղ
beef	եզի միս	branch	ճիւղ
beehive	փեթակ	brass	արոյր
before	առաջ	bread	հաց
behave	վարուիլ	breadth	լայնք
behavior	վարք	break	կոտրել
belief	հաւատք	breast	կուրծք
bell	զանգակ	breath	շունչ
beside	քով	brick	աղիւս
besides	ատկէ զատ	bride	հարս
between	միջեւ, մէջ չորեղ	bridegroom	փեսայ
bill	հաշուեցուցակ, կտուց	bridge	կամուրջ
		bright	փայլուն
bird	թռչուն	broad	լայն
birth	ծնունդ	broken	կոտրած
bit	կտոր, քիչիկ	brother	եղբայր
bite	խածնել	brow	ճակատ

bitter	դառն, լեղի	cause	պատճառ, դատ
brown	թուխ	cave	քարայր
brush	թուփ, խոզանակ,	cavity	ծակ
	վրձին	cell	բջիջ
bubble	պղպջակ	certain	ապահով, որոշ
bucket	դոյլ	certainly	անշուշտ
bud	ծիլ	chain	շղթայ
build	շինել	chair	աթոռ
building	շենք	chalk	կաւիճ
burn	այրել, այրիլ	chance	բախտ
burst	պայթել	change	փոխել, փոփո-
business	գործ, աշխատանք		խութիւն
but	բայց	charity	սէր, ողորմութիւն
butter	կարագ	chauffeur	շարժավար
button	կոճակ	cheap	աժան
by	միջոցով	cheat	խաբել, խաբեբայ
		check	արգիլել, ստուգել
		cheese	պանիր
		chemical	քիմիական
	C	chemist	քիմիապան
		chest	կուրծք
		chicken	վարեակ
cab	կառք	chief	պետ
cage	վանդակ	child	մանուկ, զաւակ
cake	կարկանդակ	chin	կզակ
calendar	օրացոյց	chorus	երգչախումբ
call	կոչ, կանչել	church	եկեղեցի
calm	հանդարտ	cigaret	ծխանիկ
canvas	պաստառ	circle	բոլորակ
capable	կարող	circumference	շրջանակ
capacity	կարողութիւն	clap	ծափ, ծափահարել
care	հոգ, հոգալ	claw	ճիրան
carriage	կառք	clean	մաքուր
carry	տանիլ	clear	յստակ
cart	սայլ	clearly	յստակօրէն
case	պարագայ,	client	յաճախորդ
	անտոմ	clock	ժամացոյց
cash	կանխիկ	cloth	կերպաս
cat	կատու	clothing	հագուստ

191

cloud	ամպ	considerate	փափկանկատ
cloudy	ամպոտ, ամպա-մած	consideration	նկատառում
		continually	շարունակաբար
coal	ածուխ	continuous	շարունակական
coat	վերարկու, բաճ-կոն	control	հակակշիռ, հա-կակշռել
cock	աքաղաղ	cook	խոհարար
coffee	սուրճ	cool	զով
cold	պաղ, ցուրտ	copper	պղինձ
collar	օձիք	copy	օրինակ, ընդօրի-նակութիւն, օրինակել
color	գոյն		
column	սիւն		
comb	սանտր	cord	չուան
come	գալ	cotton	բամպակ
comfort	հանգստութիւն	cough	հազ
comfortable	հանգստաւէտ	country	երկիր
committee	յանձնախումբ	court	դատարան, ար-քունիք
common	հասարակ		
companion	ընկեր	cover	ծածկել, ծածկոյթ
company	ընկերութիւն	covert	ծածուկ
compare	բաղդատել	cow	կով
comparison	բաղդատութիւն	crack	ճաթիլ
compete	մրցիլ	credit	պահանջ
competition	մրցում	crime	ոճիր
complain	գանգատիլ	cross	խաչ, խաչացնել
complaint	գանգատ	crown	թագ
complete	ամբողջ, կատար-եալ	crush	ջախջախել
		cruel	անգութ
complex	բարդ, բարդոյթ	cry	ապապակ, լալ
component	բաղկացուցիչ մարր	cup	գաւաթ
		cure	դարման
condition	պայման, վիճակ	current	ընթացիկ
connect	միացնել	curse	անէծք, անիծել
connection	կապակցութիւն	curtain	վարագոյր
conscience	խիղճ	curve	կոր
conscious	գիտակից	cushion	բարձ
consciousness	գիտակցութիւն	custom	սովորութիւն
consider	նկատի առնել	customhouse	մաքսատուն
considerable	մեծ, կարեւոր	cut	կտրել

D

dagger	դաշոյն
dam	շրպզել
damage	վնաս
damp	խոնաւ
dampness	խոնաւութիւն
dance	պար
danger	վտանգ
dark	մութ
date	թուական, ժամա-դրութիւն
daughter	դուստր
dawn	արշալոյս
day	օր
dead	մեռեալ
dear	սիրելի
death	մահ
debt	պարտք
decide	որոշել
decision	որոշում
decrease	պակեցնել
deem	համարել
decease,- ed	մահ, մեռած
deep	խորունկ
deficiency	պակասութիւն
deficient	պակաս
degree	աստիճան
delicate	փափուկ
demand	պահանջել
den	որջ
denomination	յարանուանու-թիւն
denominator	յատարար
dentist	ատամնաբոյժ
depend	կախում ունենալ
desert	անապատ
design	ծրագիր, նպա-տակ, ձգտրթ.

desire	փափաք, փափա-քել
destroy	քանդել
destruction	կործանում
detail	մանրամասնու-թիւն
detailed	մանրամասն
determine	որոշել
develop	զարգացնել
development	զարգացում
dew	ցօղ
diameter	տրամագիծ
differ	տարբերիլ
difference	տարբերու-թիւն
different	տարբեր
difficult	դժուար
difficulty	դժուարութիւն
digest	մարսել
digestion	մարսողութիւն
direct	ուղղակի
direction	ուղղութիւն
dirty	աղտոտ
disappear	անհետանալ
discovery	գիւտ
discount	զեղչ
disciple	աշակերտ
disease	հիւանդութիւն
disgust	պժգալ, պժգանք
dissent	համաձայն չըլլալ
distance	հեռաւորութիւն
distant	հեռու, հեռաւոր
distribute	բաժնել, բաշխել
divide	բաժնել
division	բաժանում
do	ընել
doctor	բժիշկ
doctrine	վարդապետու-թիւն
dog	շուն

dogma	դաւանանք	enough	բաւական
door	դուռ	environment	շրջապատ
doubt	տարակոյս	environs	շրջակայք
dove	տատրակ	envy	նախանձ
down	վար	equal	հաւասար
drawer	դարակ	equality	հաւասարութիւն
dream	երազ, երազել	error	սխալ
dress	հագուստ	eternal	յաւիտենական
drink	խմել, ըմպելի	eternity	յաւիտենակա-
drive	քշել, վարել		նութիւն
drop	կաթիլ	evaporate	շոգիանալ
drop	վար ձգել	even	նոյն իսկ, հարթ,
dry	չոր		դուրզ թիւ
due	պատշաճ, հասած	event	դէպք
dust, dusty	փոշի, փոշեպատ	evening	իրիկուն, երեկոյ
duty	պարտականութ.	ever	երբեք
	մաքսատուրք	every	ամէն մէկ, իւրա-
			քանչիւր
		everywhere	ամէն տեղ, ամեն-
	E		ուրեք
		evidence	ապացոյց
		evident	բացայայտ
ear	ականջ	evil	չարիք
eagle	արծիւ	exact	ճիշդ
early	կանուխ	example	օրինակ
earth	երկիր	except	բացի
east	արեւելք	exception	բացառութիւն
edge	եզերք	exchange	փոխանակութիւն,
egg	հաւկիթ		փոխանակել
effect	ազդեցութիւն	exist	գոյութիւն ունե-
effort	ճիգ		նալ
elastic	առաձգական	existence	գոյութիւն
electric	ելեքտրական	expand	տարածուիլ
elect	ընտրել	expansion	ընդարձում
election	ընտրութիւն	experience	փորձառութիւն,
emancipate	ազատագրել		ապրում
end	վախճան	experiment	փորձ
engine	մեքենայ	elect, election	փորձարկատ
engineer	ճարտարապետ,	explain	բացատրել
	մեքենավար		

export	արտածել	finger	մատ
extension	ընդլայնում	fire	կրակ, հրդեհ
eye	աչք	first	առաջին
		fish	ձուկ
		fix	հաստատել
		flag	դրօշակ
F		flame	բոց
		flat	տափակ, յարթ–
face	դեմք		բարձին
fact	եղելութիւն	flee	փախչիլ
factor	ազդակ	flesh	միս
factory	գործարան	flight	փախուստ
fail	ձախողիլ	flock	երամ
faith	հաւատք	floor	աատխատկամած
fall	ինկալ	flour	ալիւր
false	կեղծ	flow	հոսիլ
fame	համբաւ	flower	ծաղիկ
family	ընտանիք	fly	ճանճ, թռչիլ
fan	հովհար	fold	ծալք, ծալել,
far	հեռու		փաթաթ
farm	ագարակ	food	կերակուր
farmer	ագարակապան	fool	խենթ, խաբել
fast	արագ	foot	ոտք
fat	գեր	for	համար, վասն զի
fate	ճակատագիր	force	ուժ
father	հայր	forehead	ճակատ
fatigue	յոգնութիւն	forgive	ներել
fault	յանցանք	forgiveness	ներում
fear	վախ	fork	պատառաքաղ
feast	խնճոյք	form	ձեւ
feather	փետուր	former	նախկին
feeble	տկար	forsake	լքել
feel	զգալ	forward	յառաջ
feeling	զգացում	fountain	աղբիւր
female	էգ	fowl	հաւ
fertile	արգասաւոր	fox	աղուէս
fiction	վէպ	fraction	կոտորակ
field	դաշտ	frame	շրջանակ
fight	կռիւ, կռուել	free	ազատ

freedom	ազատություն	grace	շնորհ
frequent	յաճախ, յաճա-խել	graceful	շնորհալի
		grain	հատիկ
friend	բարեկամ	grammar	քերականություն
friendship	բարեկամություն	grape	խաղող
from	բացառական խնդիր է	grass	խոտ
front	ճակատ	gray	գորշ
fruit	պտուղ	great	մեծ
full	լեցուն	green	կանանչ
fume	ծուխ	grey	գորշ
future	ապագայ	grief	վիշտ
		ground	գետին
		group	խումբ
		growth	աճում
G		guarantee	երաշխաւորու-թյուն
garden	պարտէզ	guest	հիւր
gas	կազ	guide	առաջնորդ, ա-ռաջնորդել
general	ընդհանուր, գո-րավար	gun	հրացան
generation	սերունդ		
gentle	ազնիւ		
get	ստանալ	**H**	
girl	աղջիկ		
give	տալ	habit	սովորություն
glad	ուրախ	hair	մազ
glass	ապակի	ham	խոզի ապուխտ
glory	փառք	hammer	մուրճ
glove	ձեռնոց	hand	ձեռք
go	երթալ	hang	կախել
goat	այծ	happy	երջանիկ
god	աստուած	harbor	նաւահանգիստ
gold	ոսկի	hard	կարծր
good	բարի, լաւ	harmony	ներդաշնակու-թյուն
goodwill	բարի կամեցո-ղություն	hat	գլխարկ
govern	կառավարել	hate	ատել
government	կառավարություն	hatred	ատելություն
governor	կառավարիչ	have	ունենալ

196

he	ան	how	ինչպէս
head	գլուխ	husband	ամուսին
health	առողջութիւն	hygiene	առողջապահու-
healthy	առողջ		թիւն
hear	լսել		
heart	սիրտ	**I**	
heat	տաքութիւն		
heaven	երկինք	ice	սառ
heavenly	երկնային, երկ-	ice cream	պաղպաղակ
	նաւոր	idea	գաղափար
height	բարձրութիւն	ideal	իտէալ, գաղա-
hell	դժոխք		փարական
help	օգնել, օգնու-	if	եթէ
	թիւն	if not	եթէ ոչ
hen	հաւ	ill, illness	հիւանդ, հիւան-
here	այստեղ, հոս		դութիւն
heritage	ժառանգութիւն	image	պատկեր
high	բարձր	imitate	կապկել, օրի-
hill	բլուր		նակել
himself	ինքզինք	import	ներածել
hire	վարձել	importance	կարեւորութիւն
hire	վարձք	important	կարեւոր
historian	պատմաբան	improve	բարելաւել
history	պատմութիւն	impulse	մղում
hole	ծակ	in	մէջ
hollow	ծակ (ածծ.)	increase	աւելցնել
holy	սուրբ	individual	անհատ
honey	մեղր	industry	ճարտարապետուստ
honor	պատիւ	inferno, infernal	դժոխք,- ային
hook	կեռ	ink	մելան
hope	յոյս, յուսալ	insect	միջատ
horizon	հորիզոն	instinct	բնազդ
horn	եղջիւր	instrument	գործիք
horse	ձի	insurance	ապահովագրու-
hospital	հիւանդանոց		թիւն
hospitality	հիւրասիրութիւն	interest	տոկոս, շահ, շա-
hotel	պանդոկ		հագրգռութիւն
hour	ժամ	interpret	մեկնել, մեկնա-
house	տուն		բանել

197

interpretation	մեկնութիւն	kiss	համբոյր, համ-
invent	հնարել		բուրել
invest	շահարկել	knee	ծունկ, ծնրադրել
invention	դիւտ, հնարք	kneel	ծնրադրել
investigate	հետաղօտել	knife	դանակ
irregular	անկանոն	knot	կապ
irregularity	անկանոնութիւն	know	գիտնալ
iron	երկաթ	knowledge	ծանօթութիւն
island	կղզի		
ivory	փղոսկր		

L

J

		laboratory	լաբրատուծարան
		lace	ժապաւէն
jam	պտղանուշ	lad	տղայ, պատանի
jar	կարաս	lamb	գառնուկ
jaw	լղակ	lake	լիճ
jet	ինքնաթիռ	lame	կաղ
jewel	զոհար	lament	ողբալ
job	գործ	land	երկիր, ցամաք
join	միանալ, միա-	language	լեզու
	ցընել	lark	արտոյտ
journey	ճամբորդութիւն	last	վերջին
joy	հրճուանք	late	ուշ
judge	դատաւոր	latitude	լայնութիւն
juice	հիւթ	laugh	խնդալ
jump	ցատկել	laughter	խնդուք
just	արդար, ճիշդ	law	օրէնք
justice	արդարութիւն	layer	խաւ
		lead	առաջնորդել
K		leaf	տերեւ
		learning	ուսում
keep	պահել	leather	կաշի
key	բանալի	left	ձախ
kick	կիցg, կիցg նետել	leg	սրունք
kidney	երիկամ	let	թողուլ
kind	ազնիւ, տեսակ	length	երկայնութիւն
king	թագաւոր	letter	գիր, նամակ
kingdom	թագաւորութիւն	level	հարթ, հարթել

life	կեանք	mantle	վերարկու
lift	վերցնել	map	քարտէս
light	լոյս	margin	լուսանցք
like	նման, սիրել	mark	նշան
limit	սահման	market	շուկայ, հրապա-
line	գիծ		րակ
link	օղակ	married	ամուսնացած
lion	առիւծ	mass	զանգուած
lip	շրթունք	master	վարպետ, տիրա-
liquid	հեղուկ		նալ
list	ցուցակ	match	մրցում, լուցկի
little	քիչ, պզտիկ	material	նիւթ
live	ապրիլ	materialism	նիւթապաշտու-
liver	լեարդ		թիւն
living	ողջ, ապրուստ	materialist	նիւթապաշտ
load	բեռ	mature - maturity	հասուն-ութիւն
loan	փոխառութիւն	may	մայիս, կարենալ
lock	կղպել, կղպանք	me	զիս
long	երկար, երկայն	meadow	մարգագետին
longitude	երկայնութիւն	meal	կերակուր
look	նայիլ, նայ-	mean	բանլ ուզել, նշա-
	ուածք		նակել, միջին
loose	թոյլ	measure	չափ
lose	կորանցնել	meat	միս
loss	կորուստ	medical	բժշկական
loud	բարձրաձայն	medicine	դեղ
love	սէր, սիրել	meeting	ժողով
low	ցած	melody	մեղեդի
lung	թոք	melt	հալիլ, հալեցնել
		memory	յիշողութիւն
M		metal	մետաղ
		mercy	գութ, ողորմու-
machine	մեքենայ		թիւն
mad	խենթ	middle	մէջտեղ
madam	տիկին	military	զինուորական
make	շինել	milk	կաթ
male	արու	mind	միտք
man	մարդ	mine	իմս
manager	վարիչ	mineral	հանքային

minute	վայրկեան
mist	մէգ, մշուշ
mixed	խառն
mixture	խառնուրդ
modest	համեստ
money	դրամ
monkey	կապիկ
month	ամիս
moon	լուսին
morning	առաւօտ
mother	մայր
motion	շարժում
mountain	լեռ
mourn	դգալ
mouth	բերան
move	շարժիլ, շարժել
movies	շարժանկար
much	շատ
mud	ցեխ
multiply	բազմապատկել
muscle	ձնղեր
music	երաժշտութիւն, նուագ

N

nail	դամ
name	անուն
narrow	նեղ
nation	ազգ
nature	բնութիւն
natural	բնական
near	մօտ
necessary	անհրաժեշտ
neck	վիզ
needle	ասեղ
neighbor	դրացի
nerve	ջիղ

nest	բոյն
net	ցուռ, ուռկան
new	նոր
news	լուր
night	գիշեր
no	ոչ
noble	ազնիւ
noise	աղմուկ
normal	բնականոն
north	հիւսիս
northern	հիւսիսային
nose	քիթ
not	ոչ
now	հիմա
nowadays	ներկայիս
nuclear	կորիզային
nucleus	կորիզ
number	թիւ
nut	կաղին

O

oath	երդում
object	առարկայ, առար-կել
oblique	շեղ
observe	դիտել
observation	դիտողութիւն
observatory	դիտարան
of	աստուական հոլովի նախդիր
of course	անշուշտ
off	անդին, հեռու
offer	ընծայել
office	պաշտօն, պաշտօնատուն, գրասենեակ
often	յաճախ
oil	իւղ

200

old	հին, ծեր	paper	թուղթ, լրագիր
olive	ձիթապտուղ	paradise	դրախտ, արքա-յութիւն
on	վրայ		
only	միայն	parcel	ծրար
open	բաց	parallel	զուգահեռ,— ական
operation	գործողութիւն	parent	ծնողք
opinion	կարծիք	part	մաս
opposite	դիմաց	partial	մասնակի
or	կամ	particle	մասնիկ
orange	նարինջ	partner	ընկեր (գործի)
orchestra	նուագախումբ	pass	անցնիլ, արտո-
order	կարգ, հրաման		նագիր
organization	կազմակերպու-	passion	կիրք, հրայրք
	թիւն	passport	անցագիր
organize	կազմակերպել	past	անցեալ
origin	ծագում	pay	վճարել
ornament	զարդ	payment	վճարում
other	ուրիշ	peace	խաղաղութիւն
oven	փուռ	pen	գրիչ
over	վրայ, վերեւ	pencil	մատիտ
overturn	տապալել	pendulum	ճօճանակ
out	դուրս	people	ժողովուրդ
outline	ուրուագիծ,	perfume	բոյր, անուշահո-
	ուրուագծել		տութիւն
own	ունենալ	period	վերջակէտ, շրջան
owner	տէր	person	անձ
oyster	ոստրէ	personal	անձնական
ox	եզ	physical	ֆիզիքական
		piano	դաշնակ
		picture	պատկեր
	P	pigeon	աղաւնի
		pig	խոզ
page	էջ	pillar	սիւն
pain	ցաւ	pin	գնդասեղ
painful	ցաւալի	pipe	խողովակ
paint	ներկ	pity	գութ
pair	զոյգ	place	տեղ
pale	գունատ	plain	պարզ, դաշտա-
pan	տապակ		գետին

plan	ծրագիր	price	գին
plane	օդանաւ, հարթ	pride	հպարտութիւն
plant	տունկ, տնկել	priest	քահանայ
plate	պնակ	print	տպել
play	խաղալ, խաղ,	prison	բանտ
	թատերախաղ	prisoner	բանտարկեալ
please	հաճիլ, հաճեցնէք	private	անձնական
pleasure	հաճոյք	probable	հաւանական
plow	արոր, հերկել,	probability	հաւանականու-
pocket	գրպան		թիւն
poet	բանաստեղծ	produce	արտադրել
poetry	բանաստեղծու-	production	արտադրութիւն
	թիւն	profit	շահ
point	կէտ	program	յայտագիր, ծրա-
poison	թոյն		գիր
police	ոստիկանութիւն	proof	ապացոյց
policeman	ոստիկան	property	կալուած, սեփա-
policy	քաղաքականու-		կանութիւն
	թիւն, վարքագիծ	prophet	մարգարէ
political	քաղաքական	prose	արձակ
polish	յղկել, փայլեցնել	protest	բողոք, բողոքել
poor	աղքատ	public	հրապարակային
population	ժողովուրդ	pull	քաշել
pork	խոզի միս	pump	ջրհան
porter	բեռնակիր	pun	բառախաղ
position	դիրք	punish, punishment	պատժել, պատիժ
possible	կարելի	pupil	աշակերտ
possibility	կարելիութիւն	purchase	գնում, գնել
post office	նամակատուն	purpose	նպատակ
pot	անօթ	push	հրել
potato	գետնախնձոր	put	դնել
powder	փառոդ	pyramid	բուրգ
power	ուժ, զօրութիւն		
praise	գովել, գովեստ		
prayer	աղօթք	**Q**	
preach	քարոզել		
present	ներկայ	quality	յատկութիւն
press	մամուլ, ճնշել	quantity	քանակութիւն
pressure	ճնշում	queen	թագուհի

question	Հարցում	relation	յարաբերութիւն
quick	արագ	relative	յարաբերական,
quickly	արագօրէն		ազգական
quiet	հանդարտ	religion	կրօնք
quite	բոլորովին	remain	մնալ
		rent	վարձք
		reply	պատասխանել
R		represent	ներկայացնել
		reptile	սողուն
		request	խնդրել
race	ցեղ, ծիարշաւ,	resist	դիմադրել
	վազելու մրցում	resistance	դիմադրութիւն
radiate	շողարձակել	respect	յարգանք
radiation	շողարձակում	responsible	պատասխանատու
radio	ձայնասփիւում	rest	հանգիստ, հանգ-
rail	երկաթուղի		չել
rain	անձրեւ	restaurant	ճաշարան
raise	վերցնել	retail	փոքրաքանակ վա-
rapture	գմայլում		ճառում
rare	հազուագիւտ	reveal	յայտնել
rat	մուկ	revelation	յայտնութիւն
rate	սակ	reward	վարձատրութիւն
ray	ճառագայթ	rhythm	կշռոյթ
react	հակազդել	rich	հարուստ, ճոխ
reaction	հակազդեցութիւն	right	իրաւունք, չիտակ
read	կարդալ	righteous	արդար
reading	ընթերցում	ring	մատանի
ready	պատրաստ	river	գետ
reason	պատմառ, բանա-	road	ճամբայ
	կանութիւն	robe	շրջազգեստ
record	արձանագրու-	rock	ժայռ
	թիւն	roll	գլան
receipt	ստացում, ընկա-	roof	տանիք
	լագիր	room	սենեակ
red	կարմիր	root	արմատ
regret	ափսոսալ	rose	վարդ
regular	կանոնաւոր	rot	փտտիլ
regularity	կանոնաւորու-	rough	կոշտ
	թիւն	round	կլոր

203

rub	շփել	see	տեսնել
rule	կանոն	seed	հունտ
run	վազել	seem	երևալ
rush	խուժել, խուժում	select	ընտրել
		selection	ընտրութիւն
		self	անձ
	S	sell	ծախել
		send	ղրկել
sack	պարկ	sense	զգայարանք,
sad	տխուր		իմաստ
safe	ապահով	sensitive	զգայուն
safety	ապահովութիւն	separate	զատ, զատել
sage	իմաստուն	serious	լուրջ
sail	առագաստ	servant	ծառայ
saint	սուրբ	serve	ծառայել
sake (for the	...ի սիրոյն	service	ծառայութիւն
sake of)		sew	կարել
sale	վաճառում	sex	սեռ
salt	աղ	shade, shadow	շուք
same	նոյն	shake	ցնցել
sample	նմոյշ	shame	ամօթ
sand	աւազ	shape	ձև
save	փրկել, խնայել	share	բաժին
savior	փրկիչ	sharp	սուր
savor	համ	shave	ածիլել
school	դպրոց	sheep	ոչխար
science	գիտութիւն	sheet	սաւան
scientific	գիտական	shelf	դարակ
scissors	մկրատ	shell	խեցի
screw	պտուտակ	shine	փայլիլ
sea	ծով	ship	նաւ
seal	կնիք	shirt	շապիկ
search	փնտռել	shock	ցնցում
seat	նստիլ	shoe	կօշիկ
second	երկրորդ	shoot	կրակել
secondary	երկրորդական	shore	եզերք
secret	գաղտնիք, գաղտնի	short	կարճ
secretary	քարտուղար	shot	հարուած, հրացէնի
section	հատուած	show	ցուցնել

204

shower	տարափ	society	ընկերութիւն
shut	գոցել	soft	կակուղ
shutter	փեղկ	soil	հող
sick	հիւանդ	soldier	զինուոր
side	կողմ	solid	հաստատուն
sign	նշան, նշանակել	solution	լուծում, լուծոյթ
	նշանակել, ստորագրութիւն	solve	լուծել
silk	մետաքս	some	մաս մը, քիչ մը
silver	արծաթ	son	որդի
similar	նման	song	երգ
similarity	նմանութիւն	sorrow	վիշտ
simple	պարզ	sorrowful	վշտալի
simplicity	պարզութիւ	sort	տեսակ
sin	մեղք	soul	հոգի
sinful	մեղապարտ	sound	ձայն
sister	քոյր	soup	ապուր
size	մեծութիւն, չափ	south	հարաւ
skin	մորթ	southern	հարաւային
skirt	քղանցք	sow	ցանել
skull	գանկ	space	միջոց, անջրպետ
sky	երկինք	spade	բահ
slap	ապտակ	spark	կայծ
slay	սպաննել	spear	նիզակ
sleep	քնանալ	special	մասնաւոր
slide	սահիլ	specialist	մասնագէտ
slip	սահիլ	specialty	մասնագիտութիւն
slow	դանդաղ	specimen	նմոյշ
small	պզտիկ	spice	համեմ
smell	հոտ, հոտիլ,	spirit	ոգի
	հոտոտել	spiritual	ոգեկան
smile	ժպտիլ	sponge	սպունգ
smoke	ծուխ	spoon	դգալ
smooth	ողորկ	spring	զարուն, գատկել
snake	օձ	square	քառակուսի
snow	ձիւն	stable	ախոռ
so	այսպէս	stage	բեմ
soap	օճառ	stain	արատ
soar	սաւառնիլ	stamp	դրոշմաթուղթ
social	ընկերային	star	աստղ

start	．ｆ ｂ ｌ ． ｉ ｌ	subtraction	．ＨｕＡＨ ．ＳＨＩＲＵＴ
state	．ＨＳＩＨ ．ＳＨＨＨＨ ｈ ｈ ｉ ｉ ｊ ｌ	success	．ＨＳＨＨＨＨＨＵ
state	．ＨＳＨＨＨＨＨＨＨＨＨＨ	successful	．ＨＨＨＨＨ
	ＨＨＨＨＨＨＨＨＨ ．ＨＨＨＨＨ	successive	．ＨＨＨＨＨＨＨＨＨＨ
statement	．ＨＨＨＨＨＨＨＨＨＨＨＨＨＨ	such	ＨＨＨＨＨＨＨ
station	．ＨＨＨＨＨＨＨＨ	sudden	．ＨＨＨＨＨＨＨＨＨＨＨ
steal	．ＨＨＨＨＨＨ	suddenly	．ＨＨＨＨＨＨＨ
steam	．ＨＨＨＨ	sugar	．ＨＨＨＨＨ
steel	．ＨＨＨＨＨＨＨＨ	suggest	．ＨＨＨＨＨＨＨＨ
stem	．ＨＨＨＨＨＨＨＨ	suggestion	．ＨＨＨＨＨＨＨＨＨＨ
step	．ＨＨＨＨＨ	sum	．ＨＨＨＨＨ
stick	．ＨＨＨＨＨＨＨ	summer	．ＨＨＨＨ
stiff	．ＨＨＨＨＨＨＨ	sun	．ＨＨＨＨＨＨＨ ，ＨＨＨＨ
still	．ＨＨＨＨＨＨＨＨ，ＨＨＨＨ－	supply	．ＨＨＨＨＨＨＨＨＨＨ
	．ＨＨＨＨＨＨ	support	．ＨＨＨＨＨＨＨ，ＨＨＨＨＨＨ
stocking	．ＨＨＨＨＨＨＨＨ	surface	．ＨＨＨＨＨＨＨＨ
stomach	．ＨＨＨＨＨＨＨＨＨ	surprise	．ＨＨＨＨＨＨＨＨＨＨ
stone	．ＨＨＨＨ	sweet	．ＨＨＨＨＨ
stop	．ＨＨＨＨＨＨＨ	swell	．ＨＨＨＨＨＨＨ
store	．ＨＨＨＨＨＨＨＨＨ，	swelling	．ＨＨＨＨＨＨ
	．ＨＨＨＨＨＨＨ	swim	．ＨＨＨＨＨ
stork	．ＨＨＨＨＨＨＨ	sword	．ＨＨＨＨ
storm	．ＨＨＨＨＨＨＨＨ	system	．ＨＨＨＨＨＨＨＨＨＨ
story	．ＨＨＨＨＨＨＨＨＨＨＨＨ，		
	．ＨＨＨＨＨ		T
straight	．ＨＨＨＨＨＨ		
strait	．ＨＨＨＨＨＨＨ	table	．ＨＨＨＨＨＨ
strange	．ＨＨＨＨＨＨＨＨＨＨ	tail	．ＨＨＨＨ
stranger	．ＨＨＨＨＨＨＨＨＨＨ	take	．ＨＨＨＨＨＨ
stream	．ＨＨＨＨＨ	tale	．ＨＨＨＨＨＨＨＨＨＨ
street	．ＨＨＨＨＨＨＨ	talk	．ＨＨＨＨＨＨＨ
strength	．ＨＨＨＨＨＨＨＨＨＨ	tall	．ＨＨＨＨＨＨＨＨＨＨＨＨ
stretch	．ＨＨＨＨＨＨＨ	tank	．ＨＨＨＨＨＨＨＨ，
strike	．ＨＨＨＨＨＨＨ		．ＨＨＨＨＨＨＨＨ
strong	．ＨＨＨＨＨＨＨ	taste	．ＨＨＨＨＨＨ，
structure	．ＨＨＨＨＨＨＨＨ		．ＨＨＨＨＨＨＨＨＨ
subject	．ＨＨＨＨＨＨＨＨＨＨ，	tax	．ＨＨＨＨＨＨ
	．ＨＨＨＨＨＨＨＨＨ	tea	．ＨＨＨ
substance	．ＨＨＨＨＨＨ	teach	．ＨＨＨＨＨＨＨＨＨＨ

telegram	Հեռագիր	tobacco	ծխախոտ
telephone	Հեռաձայն	toe	ոտքի մատ
television	պատկերասփիւռ	together	միասին
televise	պատկերասփռել	tolerance	հանդուրժողու-
tendency	ձգտում		թիւն
tent	վրան	tomorrow	վաղը
terrace	պատշգամ	tongue	լեզու
test	փորձել	tooth	ակռայ
that	այդ, որ	top	գագաթ
the	ը, ն, (յօդ)	tortoise	կրիայ
theater	թատրոն	touch	դպչել, շօշափել
theatrical	թատերական	tough	կոշտ, կարծր
then	այն ատեն	tower	աշտարակ
theory	վարկած,	town	քաղաք
	տեսութիւն	trade	առեւտուր
there	այնտեղ	train	կառախումբ
these	այս (յոշնակի)	transparent	թափանցիկ
thick	թանձր, հաստ	transport	փոխադրել
thief	գող	travel	ճամբորդել
thin	նիհար, բարակ	tray	սկիհ
thing	բան	tree	ծառ
this	այս	trial	փորձ
thorn	փուշ	triangle	եռանկիւն
those	այդ (յոդ.)	trick	խաղ
though	թէեւ	trip	ճամբորդութիւն
thought	մտածում	trouble	նեղութիւն, նեղել
thread	թել	trousers	տաբատ
throat	կոկորդ	true	ճշմարիտ
through	մէջէն	truth	ճշմարտութիւն
throw	նետել	try	փորձել
thumb	բթամատ	turn	դառնալ
thunder	որոտում, որոտալ	twist	ոլորել
ticket	տոմս, տոմսակ		
tight	սեղմ		U
till	մինչեւ		
time	ժամանակ		
tin	թիթեղ	umbrella	հովանոց
tired	յոգնած	uncle	հօրեղբայր,
to	դէպի		մօրեղբայր

under	ստոր.		

under   ստոր.

undertake   ձեռնարկել

undoubtedly   անտարակոյս   **W**

union   միութիւն   wage   շրջավարձք

unit   միութիւն (մէկ)   waist   մէջք

universal   տիեզերական   wait   սպասել

universe   տիեզերք   wake   արթնալ

university   համալսարան   walk   քալել

until   մինչեւ   wall   պատ

unusual   անսովոր   war   պատերազմ

up   վեր   ware   անօթ

use - useful   օգուտ, օգտա-կար   warm   տաք

     wash   լուալ

usually   սովորաբար   waste   վատնել, փճացնում

     watch   դիտել, հսկել, ժամացոյց

     water, watery   ջուր, ջրոտ

     wave   ալիք

     V   wax   մեղրամոմ

     way   ճամբայ

valley   հովիտ   we   մենք

valuable   արժէքաւոր   wealth, wealthy   հարստութիւն, հարուստ

value   արժէք

vapor   շոգի   weak   տկար

veil   քող   wear   կրել, հագնիլ, մաշիլ

verse   ոտանաւոր, տա-ղաչափութիւն   weather   օդ

verve   եռանդ   web   ոստայն

vessel   նաւ, աման   week   շաբաթ

vice   մոլութիւն   weekend   շաբաթավերջ

view   տեսարան, հայեացք   weep   լալ

     weight   ծանրութիւն

violent   բուռն   well   լաւ

violet   մանիշակ, մանի-շակագոյն   west   արեւմուտք

     wet   թաց

violin   ջութակ   what   ինչ

virtue   առաքինութիւն   wheel   անիւ

vision   տեսիլք   when   երբ

voice   ձայն   whenever   երբ որ

volume   հատոր   where   ուր

wherever	ուր որ
whether	թէ
while	մինչ
whip	խարազան
whistle	սուլիչ
white	ճերմակ
who	որ, ով
whole	ամբողջ
wholesale	մեծածախական
wholesome	առողջարար
why	ինչու
wide	լայն
widow	այրի
wife	կին
wild	վայրի
will	կամք, (պիտի)
wind	հով
wind	լարել
window	պատուհան
wine	գինի
wing	թեւ
winter	ձմեռ
wire	թել, հեռագիր, հեռագրել
wise	իմաստուն
with	հետ
without	առանց
witness	վկայ
wolf	գայլ
woman	կին
wonder	զարմանք
wood	փայտ, անտառ
wool	բուրդ
word	բառ
work	գործ, աշխատութիւն

world	աշխարհ
worm	որդ
worship	պաշտել, պաշ-տամունք
wound	վէրք, վիրաւորել
wrath	զայրոյթ
write	գրել
writer	գրող, գրագէտ
writing	գրութիւն
wrong	սխալ

Y

year	տարի
yearly	տարեկան
yellow	դեղին
yes	այո
yesterday	երէկ
yoke	լուծ
yonder	անդին, այնտեղ
you	դուք
young	դեռատի, երիտասարդ
your	ձեր
youth	երիտասարդու-թիւն

Z

zeal	աւիւն
zephyr	զեփիւռ
zero	զերո
zest	եռանդ

Other Regional Interest Titles from Hippocrene Books

The Art of Persian Cooking

This collection of 200 recipes introduces readers to the cuisine of Iran and such neighbors as Turkey, Armenia, and Azerbaijan. It features such traditional Persian dishes as Abgushte Adas (Lentil Soup), Mosamme Khoreshe (Eggplant Stew), and Lamb Kebab.

190 pages • 5½ x 8½ • ISBN 0-7818-0241-5 • W • $9.95pb • (125)

A Taste of Turkish Cuisine

This cookbook's 187 recipes feature the traditional dishes of Turkey, which make use of a variety of beans, herbs, grains, vegetables, and fresh fruits, as well as one of Turkey's most important contributions to international cuisine, yogurt. Simple yet rich in flavors, Turkish cooking is resonant of its varied influences, which range from Chinese and Mongolian dishes to those of Persia and Greece.

273 pages • 6 x 9 • 2-Color • ISBN 0-7818-0948-7 • W • $24.95hc • (392)

The Art of Uzbek Cooking

A historical crossroads in Central Asia, Uzbekistan and its cuisine reflect the range of nationalities that form the country and continue to flourish there. This collection of 175 authentic Uzbek recipes provides an introduction to a little known and exciting cuisine through easy-to-follow recipes that have been tested and adapted for use in North American kitchens.

280 pages • 6 x 9 • b/w illustrations • ISBN 0-7818-0669-0 • W • $24.95hc • (767)

Armenian-English/English-Armenian (Eastern) Concise Dictionary
9,000 entries • 380 pages • 4 x 6 • ISBN 0-7818-0150-8 • W • $12.95pb • (490)

Eastern Armenian-English/English-Eastern Armenian Dictionary and Phrasebook
4,500 entries • 232 pages • 3¾ x 7 • ISBN 0-7818-1006-X • W • $11.95pb • (1)

Azerbaijani-English/English-Azerbaijani
Dictionary and Phrasebook
4,000 entries • 174 pages • 3¾ x 7 • ISBN 0-7818-0684-4 • $11.95pb • (753)

Farsi-English/English-Farsi Concise Dictionary
8,000 entries • 250 pages • 4 x 6 • ISBN 0-7818-0860-X • $12.95pb • (260)

Georgian-English/English-Georgian Dictionary & Phrasebook
1,300 entries • 174 pages • 3¾ x 7 • ISBN 0-7818-0542-2 • $11.95pb • (630)

Turkish-English/English-Turkish Dictionary & Phrasebook
2,500 pages • 228 pages • 3¾ x 7½ • ISBN 0-7818-0904-5 • $11.95pb • (230)

Uzbek-English/English-Uzbek Concise Dictionary
7,500 entries • 329 pages • 4 x 6 • ISBN 0 7818 0165 6 • $11.95pb • (4)

Uzbek-English/English-Uzbek Dictionary & Phrasebook
3,000 entries • 200 pages • 3¾ x 7½ • ISBN 0-7818-0959-2 • $11.95pb • (166)

Hippocrene Beginner's Series

The Beginner's series consists of basic language instruction, which includes vocabulary, grammar, and review exercises. The books also include cultural insights, historical material, and facts about everyday living, including shopping, eating out, and numerous other topics.

Arabic for Beginners
Revised Edition
204 pages • 5½ x 8½ • ISBN 0-7818-0841-3 • $11.95pb • (229)

Beginner's Assyrian
185 pages • 5 x 9 • ISBN 0-7818-0677-1 • $11.95pb • (763)

Beginner's Bulgarian
207 pages • 5½ x 8½ • ISBN 0-7818-0300-4 • $9.95pb • (76)

Beginner's Chinese *with 2 Audio CDs*
200 pages • 2 enclosed CDs • 5½ x 8½ • ISBN 0-7818-1095-7 • $21.95pb • (174)

Intermediate Chinese *with Audio C*
300 pages • 1 enclosed CD • 5½ x 8½ • ISBN 0-7818-0996-5 • $21.95pb • (186)

Beginner's Czech
200 pages • 5½ x 8½ • 0-7818-0231-8 • ISBN 0-7818-0231-8 • $9.95pb • (74)

Beginner's Dari
250 pages • 5½ x 8½ • ISBN 0-7818-1012-4 • $16.95pb • (233)
Beginner's Finnish
200 pages • 5½ x 8½ • ISBN 0-7818-1024-8 • $14.95pb • (492)

Beginner's French
478 pages • 5½ x 8½ • ISBN 0-7818-0863-4 • $16.95pb • (264)

Beginner's Greek
200 pages • 5½ x 8½ • ISBN 0-7818-1001-9 • $16.95pb • (287)

Beginner's Hungarian
Revised Edition
166 pages • 5½ x 8½ • ISBN 0-7818-0866-9 • $14.95pb • (308)

Beginner's Irish
145 pages • 5½ x 8½ • ISBN 0-7818-0784-0 • $14.95pb • (320)

Beginner's Italian
192 pages • 5½ x 8½ • ISBN 0-7818-0839-1 • $14.95pb • (208)

Beginner's Japanese
290 pages • 5½ x 8½ • ISBN 0-7818-0234-2 • $11.95pb • (53)

Beginner's Lithuanian
326 pages • 5½ x 8½ • ISBN 0-7818-0678-X • $19.95pb • (764)

Beginner's Maori
121 pages • 5½ x 8½ • ISBN 0-7818-0605-4 • $8.95pb • (703)

Beginner's Polish
200 pages • 5½ x 8½ • ISBN 0-7818-0299-7 • $9.95pb • (82)

Beginner's Romanian
232 pages • 5½ x 8½ • 0-7818-0208-3 • ISBN 0-7818-0208-3 • $7.95pb • (79)

Beginner's Russian
200 pages • 5½ x 8½ • ISBN 0-7818-0232-6 • $9.95pb • (61)

Beginner's Serbo-Croatian
257 pages • 6 x 8¾ • ISBN 0-7818-0845-6 • $14.95pb • (138)

Beginner's Slovak
180 pages • 5 x 7 • ISBN 0-7818-0815-4 • $14.95pb • (534)

Beginner's Spanish
315 pages • 5½ x 8½ • ISBN 0-78180840-5 • $14.95pb • (225)

Beginner's Swedish
262 pages • 5½ x 8½ • ISBN 0-7818-0951-7 • $14.95pb • (383)

Beginner's Turkish
200 pages • 5½ x 8½ • ISBN 0-7818-0679-8 • $14.95pb • (765)

Beginner's Vietnamese
517 pages • 7 x 10 • ISBN 0-7818-0411-6 • $19.95pb • (253)

Prices subject to change without notice. To purchase Hippocrene Books, contact your local bookstore, call (718) 454-2366, or write to: HIPPOCRENE BOOKS, 171 Madison Avenue, New York, NY 10016. Please enclose check or money order, adding $5.00 shipping (UPS) for the first book, and $.50 for each additional book.